SUPERMARKETS TRANSFORMED

Understanding Organizational
and Technological Innovations

JOHN P. WALSH

D0075375

RUTGERS UNIVERSITY PRESS
New Brunswick, New Jersey

Copyright © 1993 by John P. Walsh

All rights reserved

Manufactured in the United States of America

Library of Congress Cataloging-in-Publication Data

Walsh, John P., 1962–
    Supermarkets transformed : understanding organizational and
technological innovations / John P. Walsh.
       p. cm. — (The Arnold and Caroline Rose monograph series of
the American Sociological Association)
    Includes bibliographical references and index.
    ISBN 0-8135-1969-1
    1. Supermarkets—United States—Management. 3. Grocery trade—
United States—Technological innovations. 4. Grocery trade—United
States—Management. I. Title. II. Series   HF5469.23.U62W35   1993
658.8'78—dc20   92-35961
                                                                CIP

British Cataloging-in-Publication information available

HF
5469.23
.U62
W35
1993

For John P. Walsh, Sr.

CONTENTS

List of Figures   *ix*

List of Tables   *xi*

Acknowledgments   *xiii*

1   Introduction   *1*

2   Environmental Changes during the Postwar Period   *41*

3   The Degradation of Work?: The Meatcutters   *59*

4   Computerization in the Supermarkets   *89*

5   Diversification and Its Effects on the Shop Floor   *107*

6   Conclusion   *149*

Notes   *165*

Bibliography   *169*

Name Index   *179*

Subject Index   *182*

LIST OF FIGURES

Figure 1.1. Organizational Chart for a Conventional Store   8

Figure 1.2. Organizational Chart for a Superstore   10

Figure 1.3. A Politicized Context Model of Innovation   18

Figure 1.4. Workers' Responses to Innovations in Their Bundle of
Tasks   29

Figure 2.1. Average Wages (Current Dollars per Hour) in the
Grocery Industry, 1954–1990   43

Figure 2.2. Net Profit as a Percentage of Sales, Supermarket
Industry, 1959–1984   44

Figure 2.3. Net Profit as a Percentage of Sales, SuperStores,
1959–1984   44

Figure 2.4. Percentage of Total Grocery Store Sales by Firm Size,
1948–1987   57

LIST OF TABLES

Table 1.1. Sales and Employment for Selected Industries, 1977, 1982, and 1987   5

Table 1.2. Percentage of Stores Offering Various Service Departments, 1970–1990   11

Table 1.3. Breakdown of Interviews by Department, Sex, Age, and Seniority   34

Table 1.4. Sex Distribution by Department (All Employees for Two Stores)   35

Table 2.1. Population, Urbanization, and Average Grocery Store Sales, 1940–1990   43

Table 2.2. Female Labor Force Participation Rates, by Marital Status   45

Table 2.3. Median Hours Open per Week and Percentage Open Sundays for Supermarkets, 1975–1990   49

Table 2.4. Convenience Stores Sales and Stores as a Percentage of Total Grocery Sales and Stores, 1965–1990   50

Table 3.1. Wage Rates among Unionized Grocery Workers, 1971–1979 (Current Dollars per Hour)   67

Table 3.2. Concentration Ratios in Meat Packing and Retail Food, 1947–1987   71

Table 3.3. Production Figures for Frozen Meat, Frozen Food, and All Meat, 1950–1969 (Millions of Pounds)   73

Table 3.4. A Comparison of Handling Costs for Boxed and
Hanging Beef   *81*

Table 4.1. Responses by Department Heads to the Question:
"What Is the Most Difficult Part of Your Job?" (Open Ended)   *103*

Table 5.1. Supermarket Delis Containing Hot Food Cases, by
Region   *115*

Table 5.2. Responses to the Question: "How Did You Learn to
Do Your Job?" (Open Ended)   *137*

Table 5.3. Regression of Wages in Supermarkets (Standard Errors
in Parentheses)   *144*

ACKNOWLEDGMENTS

WHILE THE TITLE page lists only one author, this work is the result of the interaction of a large number of people. I would like to thank all those people, without whom this book would not exist.

I'll begin by acknowledging my debt to my respondents for their cooperation. I am always pleasantly surprised at the public's willingness to participate in social research. Some were particularly helpful. Unfortunately, confidentiality prevents me from singling them out. You know who you are.

There is also a large number of people who commented on this book in one form or another. Many thanks to Carlos Aguilar, William Bielby, William Bridges, Wesley Cohen, Tom Finholt, William Finlay, Alfred Jablonski, John Lammers, Robin Leidner, James Norr, Anthony Orum, Charles Perrow, and Paula Rossow. James Zetka was particularly helpful and deserves special thanks. Arthur Stinchcombe and Howard Becker gave me substantial assistance in turning my proposal into a dissertation. One of the critical components of an apprenticeship is watching good craftsmen work. I hope that I have learned from their examples. Mildred Schwartz was instrumental in turning the dissertation into a book. Teresa Sullivan at the Rose Monograph Series was helpful and encouraging. Thanks also to Marlie Wasserman at Rutgers University Press. Several anonymous reviewers gave me extensive comments, and I hope to thank them in person some day.

Perhaps my greatest intellectual debt is to Ackie Feldman. Ackie is the linchpin for what may be called the Northwestern School of sociology. His prodding and patience combined to challenge me to discover what great truths could be found by talking to deli clerks and reading *Progressive Grocer.* I'm not sure if any great truths were uncovered, but I did find a few interesting things.

I would like to thank the Graduate School at Northwestern University, the National Science Foundation, and the National Institute of Mental Health for keeping me alive while I worked on this. Thanks also to the editors of *Sociological Quarterly* for letting me reprint parts of an article they previously published.

Finally, I would like to thank my best friend, Anne. She has put up with many years of graduate school disease while I finished this study. She also doesn't mind if I spend way too much time shopping. Her love and support made this book possible. Thank you, Anne.

Chicago, 1992

SUPERMARKETS TRANSFORMED

1

INTRODUCTION

IN JULY 1951, *Progressive Grocer*, a leading industry trade journal, featured an article on the Food Basket store outside of New Haven, Connecticut (*PG* July 1951). The six checkout stands of the 6,000-square-foot store rang up more than $800,000 in sales per year. The totally self-service store was divided into grocery, produce, dairy, frozen food, and meat departments, with prices clearly marked on almost every item. Butchers cut the meat and then passed it on to the women who wrapped it and filled the cases. The meat department also included a self-service delicatessen for cold cuts. The store also had a separate, 70-square-foot section for drugs and magazines.

In November 1984, *Progressive Grocer*'s store-of-the-month was the Minyard Food Store outside of Dallas (*PG* November 1984). In its 46,000 square feet, there were several specialty service departments, including a deli; a bakery; a cheese, pasta and pizza combination; a florist's shop; a service seafood shop; a service cosmetics counter; a pharmacy; and a bank. The store offered carryout service to all customers. The deli and bakery preparation areas were exposed, allowing customers to see women baking bread or making sandwiches. There was also a seating area where shoppers could stop for coffee or a sandwich. Three-quarters of the baked goods were prepared from scratch, the rest were baked from frozen dough. Together, the deli and bakery accounted for 4.5% of total store sales, almost $1 million per year. The full-service seafood department emphasized answering customers' questions about preparing seafood and brought in

2.5% of total store volume. The cosmetics counter and pharmacy were part of the department that carried health and beauty aids and nonfoods. The 90 full-time and 108 part-time employees provided all of this service, as well as stocking and maintaining the store. The 12 checkout stands scanned, from computer-coded symbols, more than $20 million worth of products per year.

IN A PERIOD of just over one generation, supermarkets have changed from small, often family-owned, stores specializing in a limited number of grocery and meat items to enormous retail centers that include not only larger selections in the traditional grocery, meat, produce, and dairy departments but also substantially expanded nonfood and general merchandise sections and an increasing number of specialty shops, such as delis, bakeries, seafood shops, and florists. These changes include new technologies in the stores, new ways of organizing the work in the stores, and changes in the shopping habits of customers. They are a response to demographic, economic, and cultural changes that have transformed the United States during the last 40 years.

Technology has changed supermarkets through the introduction of machines that mechanize or automate some in-store tasks. For example, in the meat department firms have introduced power saws for cutting meat and machines that wrap and price meat. At the front end, they have introduced electronic cash registers and computerized scanners that automatically match an item to its price. Firms have also computerized ordering. Thus, like many other industries, retail food has taken advantage of technological advances to mechanize or even automate many of the tasks that were previously done by hand. By exploring the process by which these new technologies have become part of standard practice in the industry, we will increase our understanding of the subtleties of technological change in an organizational context.

There have also been impressive changes in the organization of work in the stores. In the 1930s and 1940s, there was the change to self-service in grocery stores, which shifted much of the in-store work from the clerks to the customers (Zimmerman 1955, Glazer

1984). In the meat department there was an extensive effort over several decades to centralize the processing of meat. There was also tremendous growth in store size, as the opening comparison illustrates. These larger stores included a wide variety of new specialty shops and required workers who specialized in numerous tasks (e.g., cooking, baking, floral design) that were not part of the work of store clerks in the previous generation. Finally, there was a change in the division of labor between shop-floor employees and managers. As store size increased, there was an increasing decentralization, first to the store managers and then to the shop-floor employees (cf. Lawrence 1958). Like technological innovation, organizational innovation is a complicated process. There has been substantial recent interest in modifying existing organizations to make them more competitive. This book analyzes the details of organizational innovations to develop a model that accounts for the complexity of the process.

These changes have been driven in part by changes in the environments in which supermarkets operate. There have been several major cultural changes that have had important impacts on the organization of supermarkets. The biggest change has been the increase in the number of women who work outside the home. This development has led to an increased demand for service, including staying open longer hours and offering more prepared foods. There has also been a slowdown in population growth, which has increased competitive pressure on the firms. Finally, there have been changes in eating habits. Firms have responded to the changes in several ways. At the firm level, they have begun to increase chain size and market shares. They have also tried to cut costs, particularly for labor, through technological innovations. In addition, firms have begun to provide more and more services and to change their product mix to match the new preferences. Several of the organizational innovations have been a direct or indirect result of these changes in demand.

How did this transformation of the retail food industry come about? Why did supermarkets adopt certain innovations and not others? What determines the final form of a successful innovation? How have these changes affected those who work in this industry? What insights do these changes give us into the nature of work over the last 40 years? What can these changes in supermarkets tell us about organizational change in general? These are the questions this book addresses through an analysis of the various major innovations in supermarkets over the last 40 years.

IN MANY WAYS, the ideal example of modern capitalism is not the factory, nor even the stock market, but the supermarket. For example, the movie *Moscow on the Hudson,* a comic look at the United States from the perspective of an immigrant from the Soviet Union, caricatures the U.S. economy by showing scenes from a supermarket and a department store. Retail trade has become an increasingly important part of the total economy, and retail food has become an increasingly important part of retail trade. In 1987, retail trade accounted for almost 22% of total employment, about the same as all manufacturing industries (US Census 1991). There were more than 18 million employees in retail trade in 1987. The supermarket industry is a growing subset of the retail trade sector of the economy. Retail food stores employed more than 3.1 million workers in 1988, an increase of over 60% since 1970 (US BLS 1984, US BLS 1987, US BLS 1990). Total grocery sales in 1990 were $369 billion, and the largest firms in the industry each had sales of over $10 billion (*PG* April 1991). The largest firms in the industry also average sales of $10 million per store (*PG* October 1984). So even at the store level these are substantial economic entities.

Table 1.1 compares sales and employment for retail food, auto, steel, and machine-tools industries for the years 1977, 1982, and 1987. The table shows that while employment in auto, steel, and machine tools all declined during this period, employment in retail food increased and in 1987 was over 10 times that of auto or steel and 60 times that of machine tools. Sales in the retail food industry were nearly twice the sales for the three heavy industries combined. This table suggests the importance of the retail food industry in the current economy. The table also mirrors the more general trend in the U.S. economy of a shift away from manufacturing and toward service industries. Because of this centrality in the U.S. economy, retail food firms are likely to reflect the major changes in the economy during this period.

Table 1.1. Sales and Employment for Selected Industries, 1977, 1982, and 1987

Industry	Sales ($Billions)			Employment (Thousands)		
	1977	1982	1987	1977	1982	1987
Retail Food	158.4	246.1	301.8	1,964	2,348	2,855
Auto	76.5	70.7	133.3	344	240	281
Steel and Iron	39.7	53.3	27.1	452	289	163
Machine Tools	3.9	5.8	4.6	83	78	46

Sources: US Census, 1985:764, 766, 769, 779; US Census, 1987:1–14, 1–15; US Census, 1990:755, 769.

The supermarket can also be seen as a minipolity. Because supermarkets are so central to the economy, they can become the focus of political actions, by the workers, by the managers, and by the consumers. For example, when price scanners were introduced, workers, customers, grocers, and computer firms each argued for the adoption of a system favorable to their group's interests. The final solution was a compromise that considered the interests of each of these sets of actors. Similarly, much consumer action is targeted at supermarkets, where inflation, tainted product, or other consumer issues are most visibly manifest. So, for example, retail food was one of the last industries exempted from the wage-and-price controls implemented by the Nixon administration.

Finally, in addition to their economic and political importance, supermarkets can be seen as central to modern American culture. From the point of view of consumers, the supermarket is the embodiment of the basic American values of consumption and affluence (rivaled perhaps by the shopping mall). The sorry state of grocery stores in the Soviet Union, with their long lines, limited selection, and scarcity of goods, was offered as a constant reminder of how much more successful the American economy was than its socialist counterpart. Major cultural shifts, such as the suburbanization of the postwar period, the increase in the number of women working during the last few decades, the upscaling of consumption during the Reagan years, were all reflected in the supermarkets of the period. During the 1950s stores moved to the suburbs and added large parking lots. During the 1970s stores added more convenience foods and more services. During the 1980s, firms included elaborate and exotic product mixes (particularly in the produce section), and even more services.

Supermarkets also reflect the changing culture of work in the United States. Supermarkets grew along with other service industries as the economy shifted from manufacturing to service. Union strength in the supermarkets, like that in much of the economy, reached its peak in the mid-1970s; membership and influence have steadily declined since then. Finally, along with firms in many other industries, supermarket firms began to recognize the importance of worker input into the decision-making process.

Economically, politically, and culturally, supermarkets are the locus of many of the changes in the United States during the last half century. As the general prosperity and growth of the postwar period gave way to the increasingly competitive and uncertain economy of the 1970s and 1980s, firms across the nation began to search for answers to the question of how best to compete in the current market. The answer that many successful firms (and the management theorists who studied these firms) settled upon was that innovation was an important strategy for success. By following the history of innovation in supermarkets, we can gain some useful insights into the nature of innovation and, in particular, learn more about how ideas move from being new inventions to becoming standard practice in the industry.

Much of the recent scholarly attention has focused on how to create firms that will generate lots of new ideas (cf. Kanter 1983, Ouchi 1981, Peters and Waterman 1982, Pinchot 1985). This book, by contrast, will concentrate on the uncertain process of incorporating new ideas into the work routines of an organization. From a management point of view, this analysis will generate insights into how best to introduce an innovation into the organization. By being aware of potential sources of resistance, managers can incorporate this knowledge into their innovation strategy. For example, by being sensitive to the importance of certain tasks for a given occupation, managers can design innovations that improve productivity but do not generate worker resistance. From a policy point of view, this analysis can make suggestions that will facilitate the incorporation of new ideas into standard practice. For example, committees that facilitate cooperation and shared standards between an industry and its suppliers can also greatly facilitate the innovation process. Finally, for sociologists, this analysis will help specify the process by which organizations change. In particular, by focusing on the open-systems nature of organizations and on the political contingencies of that system, the book develops a model of innovation that is more complete than previous work in the economics and sociology of innovation.

The Organization of the Modern Supermarket

The retail food industry has gone through a tremendous transformation since World War II. The most obvious change has been the great increase in store size. As store size has increased, so has the complexity of the division of labor in the store. This section gives an overview of how the changes noted above have affected the organization of work in the supermarkets.

Figure 1.1 shows a typical organizational chart for a store of the 1950s and 1960s, a store like the one described at the beginning of the chapter. Such a store might have had 20 to 60 employees. The jobs in boxes are management jobs. The store management consisted of a store manager and a comanager. Their function was to take care of the store's finances, supervise the employees, allocate hours for scheduling, and plan store pricing, ordering, and display.

Below the managers are listed the various department heads: meat, produce, grocery, and front end. Their duties were to supervise, order, and schedule for their departments. They also did the stocking and production work for their departments, along with the stockers, clerks, cutters, and wrappers. Department heads were a hybrid between a foreman and a gang boss. They were hourly employees but had set schedules and were guaranteed 40 hours work per week. Their wages were determined not by seniority but by store sales. They were supervisors but were members of the union in unionized stores. The position of department head stretched the concepts of management and labor, since the department head was both a manager and a worker.

Below the department heads were (in the meat department) the

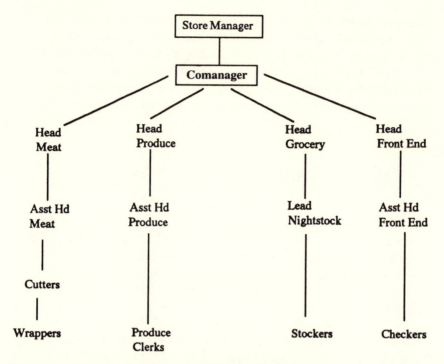

Figure 1.1. Organizational Chart for a Conventional Store
Jobs in boxes (e.g., Store Manager) are management positions. Department heads (e.g., Head Meat) are not management positions.

cutters and (for all the departments) the various clerks: stockers, checkers, produce clerks, and meat wrappers. They worked with the department heads to perform the various tasks in the store: unloading the trucks and stocking the shelves, pricing product, running the cash registers, bagging groceries, building displays, processing meat, cleaning, and assisting customers.

During the last 40 years, retail food chains have followed a diversification strategy of expanding into new geographic and product markets. The firm I studied most closely, which I refer to as Super-Stores, currently operates in 20 states. Individual stores became not only larger but also increasingly diversified. As store size increased, there emerged during the 1970s a new kind of store, the superstore.

The superstore typically has between 80 and 150 employees, although some have as many as 500 employees. The new stores stock more than 25,000 different items compared to an average of 5,000 to 8,000 items per store in the 1950s and 1960s. Figure 1.2 shows the organizational chart for a typical superstore. Again, jobs in boxes are management jobs. Jobs in boldface, underlined type are new jobs—jobs not found in the older, smaller stores. The store manager and comanager have been replaced by a unit manager and several functional managers: perishables, grocery-nonfoods, and front end. The unit manager (the store manager for a superstore) oversees store planning, promotion, and employee evaluations and supervises the functional managers. The functional managers are in charge of supervising and planning for their departments. This is a hierarchical division of labor of the management functions, with direct supervision by the functional managers and planning by the unit manager. This change created at the store level a structure similar to the firm-level multidivisional structure adopted by most firms during the postwar era (Chandler 1962, Fligstein 1985).

Below the functional managers are the department heads. As store size increased, new departments and new department heads were added, including those for the deli, seafood, and nonfoods departments. As Table 1.2 shows, there has been a tremendous increase in the number of stores with these specialty shops. For example, in 1970, only 24% of stores had delis and only 26% had bakeries. By 1990, 73% of stores had delis and 56% had bakeries. Among the larger stores (those with more than $12 million annual sales), 85% have delis. This strategy of increasing product lines, particularly service products, has become the dominant strategy in the industry. One store I observed not only had a deli (with a restaurant), a bakery, and a seafood shop but also an ice cream parlor, video shop, pharmacy, bank, wine cellar, florist, nutrition center, juice bar, perfume counter, photo lab, and toy section. It catered receptions, provided flowers for weddings, decorated cakes, and made keys (see also Fleet 1985, *Forbes* 1982, *Newsweek* 1986, *Newsweek* 1988, *New York Times* 1986, *New York Times* 1989). These are not trivial sidelines. During one Easter weekend, for example, this store sold $25,000 worth of flowers. In fact, SuperStores is one of the country's largest florists. These new department heads have the same functions as the old ones, but over

9

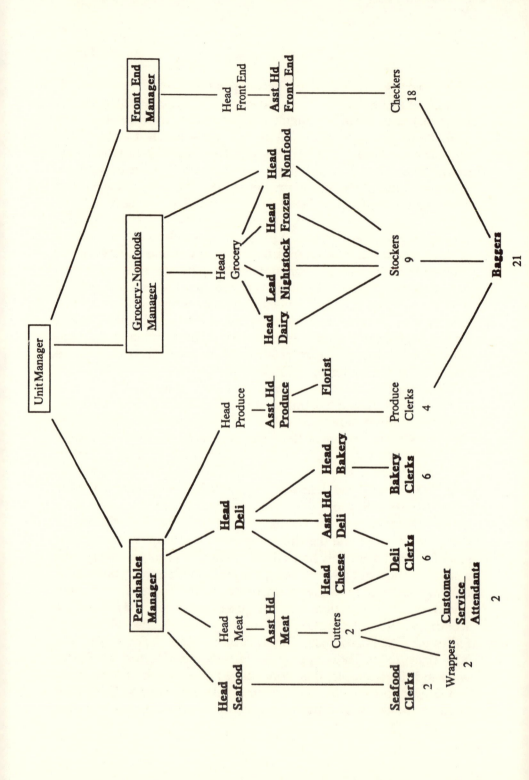

Table 1.2. Percentage of Stores Offering Various Service Departments, 1970–1990

Services Offered	1970	1972	1974	1976	1978	1980	1982	1984	1986	1988	1990
Deli	24	24	37	33	40	42	50	51	60	71	73
Bakery	26	25	35	32	40	39	47	53	60	65	56
Bakeoff*	16	15	19	20	26	24	30	34	38	44	27
Scratch*	10	10	16	12	14	15	17	19	22	21	29
Seafood	NA**	NA	NA	NA	NA	NA	17	23	23	32	33
Florals	NA	NA	36	65	66	60	42	54	62	NA	52

Source: *PG, Annual Reports*, various years.
*Bakeoff bakeries are in-store bakeries which cook from frozen dough. Scratch bakeries are bakeries that cook from dough prepared in the store.
**NA—not available.

products that were not previously part of the store. This is an aggregation of labor rather than division of labor, because more tasks were included in the organization. Chapters 3 and 5 will explore the development of these diversification innovations.

In addition, new subordinate department heads were added for the meat, front end, deli, produce, dairy, frozen food departments, and for night stocking. As the departments grew, the tasks of the department head became too numerous for one person. The assistants primarily took care of supervising and ordering when the department head was not available, either because that person was absent or because the stores stayed open more hours.

The department heads of the smaller departments (bakery, dairy, frozen food, cheese, floral) took care of the production as well as ordering and supervising for their departments. As department size increased, these smaller departments were created to take advantage of the specialized knowledge that could be developed by concentrating on a smaller group of similar products such as frozen food,

Figure 1.2. Organizational Chart for a Superstore
Jobs in boxes (e.g., Unit Manager) are management positions. Department heads (e.g., Head Meat) are not management positions. Job titles that are underscored and boldface (e.g., Seafood Clerk) are new jobs (cf. Figure 1.1). Numbers represent the number of incumbents for a given job in a typical SuperStore. All jobs without numbers have exactly one incumbent.

cheese, or floral items. Again the division of labor was hierarchical, with the subdepartments concentrating on a small part of what had once been one large department: grocery, meat, or produce.

There was also the development of a new category of low-status workers, who specialized in such tasks as bagging and cleaning. The bagger was a hierarchical division of labor similar to the introduction of orderlies in the hospital to do the cleaning tasks that had previously been a responsibility of nurses (Hughes 1984, ch. 30). In the superstores, the various clerks could now concentrate on stocking and in many cases, ordering, because they were freed from the low-status work of bagging and cleaning (see Chapter 4). As Figure 1.2 shows, the bagger is the entry-level position for all jobs other than the meat department.

Thus, over the last several decades, grocery stores have changed from fairly small, relatively simple organizations to fairly large and complicated economic entities. The following section will explore previous research on changes in organizations and the labor process to develop a theory that will explain this transformation.

Innovations in Organizations

This study will attempt to answer the question, how did supermarkets change from the form depicted in Figure 1.1 to that depicted in Figure 1.2? More generally, what are the sources of changes in the organization of work? The following sections explore the dominant theories of the sources of innovation in the workplace.

Technology

Some analysts have argued that the transformation of the workplace is driven by technological innovations. For example, Braverman (1974) has argued that firms introduce a variety of technological innovations to eliminate worker skills and thereby transfer control over the labor process from workers to managers. As early as 1911, Taylor had argued that firms can increase productivity and reduce their dependence on workers by increasing the division of labor and mechanizing much of the work. Similarly, Edwards (1979) has argued that the drive by managers to control labor led to the introduction of machine-based systems of control. This technical control allows managers to control the actions of the workers without directly supervising and coercing them. It also eliminates the need for many of the workers' skills and much of their autonomy.

Although a variety of technological innovations has transformed the labor process in supermarkets over the last 40 years, my data show only minimal support for the deskilling thesis. Most of the innovations cited were attempts to move into new markets or to reduce production costs in old markets (generate monopoly profits). These changes sometimes resulted in increased worker control and sometimes in decreased worker control. Only one change (centralization of meat cutting) appears to follow Braverman's model of an innovation explicitly designed to wrest control away from skilled craftsmen (see Chapter 3). Even in this case, economic gains motivated the change. Many of the changes explicitly increased workers' control and involvement in the work process. Why is there not more evidence for Braverman's thesis? I argue that the answer lies in the organizational implications of his thesis. The next section outlines the theoretical background for that argument.

Environment

In addition to the importance of technological innovations, many authors have pointed out that changes in work are often the result of environmental pressures on the organization. Perrow (1967) notes that there should be a match between the amount of variation in the work, or the uncertainty of the work process, and the amount of skill of the worker. Similarly, the contingency theories of organizational structure note that organizations should match their structures to the types of environments they face (Lawrence and Lorsch 1967, Galbraith 1973). If there is a lot of variability or uncertainty in the environment, firms should decentralize decision making, and conversely, in the face of stable environments, firms should centralize decision making for increased efficiency. Chandler (1962), for example, argues that as firms moved into more complicated environments, they adopted the more decentralized multidivisional form structure. This relationship between structure and environment can be understood using an information processing model of organizations (March and Simon 1958, Stinchcombe 1990). As firms become more heterogeneous, managers begin to suffer problems of bounded rationality (Williamson 1985). The volume of decisions that has to be made at a given level becomes too great for one person. In addition, the necessary information and the skills to process and interpret that information for at least some of the decisions are outside the domain of the manager at that level (Simon 1976). By decentralizing decision making, the firm presents each of its employees with a manageable volume of decisions and with decisions that are in that person's domain, overcoming the limits on rationality (Child 1977). In addition, using skilled workers (i.e., those with more information-processing capabilities) at the points of high uncertainty helps to further increase efficiency (Stinchcombe 1990, ch. 2). However, as Williamson notes, such decentralized firms must develop governance structures that will prevent opportunism.

Several theorists, particularly those with a more applied interest in organizational theory, have argued that decentralized organizational forms are increasingly necessary. As U.S. hegemony in world markets declines and, more importantly, as firms in the domestic market are less buffered from environmental uncertainty, they must become increasingly responsive to changes in consumer preferences, technologies of production, and innovations by competitors. Piore and Sabel (1984) argue that the large, centralized firm with a highly routinized production process is becoming less viable in the highly variable and highly competitive world market of the late twentieth century. They propose an alternative organizational form, which they call flexible specialization, which consists of networks of skilled workers using general-purpose tools that can be adapted to various production processes. They claim that flexible specialization is more efficient under current conditions of competition and change. By encouraging competition but limiting that competition to either product or production innovations (instead of, for example, cutting wages), such industrial districts encourage innovation, which helps them stay competitive. Peters and Waterman (1982) and Ouchi

(1981), after studying large, successful U.S. firms, argue that those firms that have been most successful in recent years are those that have managed to decentralize decision making to take advantage of the flexibility such structures provide.

The move toward more decentralized organizational forms has important implications for the organization of work in those firms. Such decentralized structures depend on having skilled workers at the decision-making nodes in the organization. If the environment is such that there is substantial uncertainty or variation at the lowest levels of the organization—at the level of the production process or firm-client interaction—then these workers must have the skills necessary to react appropriately to these changes (Perrow 1967). Ouchi's Theory Z (1981) emphasizes the importance of worker cooperation and worker input into the production process for organizational success. Such mechanisms as quality circles allow firms to take advantage of the accumulated wisdom of workers (Cole 1985). Pinchot (1985) argues for giving employees the freedom to innovate new product-service lines (intrapreneuring), to take advantage of the synergies created when innovative employees act in a large organization. Because of the inalienability of service from the worker providing the service, service firms are particularly dependent on the quality of their work force and therefore should invest in increasing worker skills and in incorporating worker knowledge into the firm's practice (Heskett 1986).

Thus, the literature on organizations and their environments and recent management theory suggests that firms are moving toward more decentralized organizational structures. These firms increasingly rely on skilled, autonomous workers to implement their organizations' goals. This theory implies a very different set of expectations about the nature of work from the deskilling thesis. Rather than assuming increased centralization and routinization of work, the contingency theory of organization, coupled with an assumption of increased uncertainty in the current world market, suggests that work should become more autonomous and skilled, as firms attempt to shorten information flows and to compete in multiple environments.

Our analysis of changes in the supermarket industry will allow us to compare these two models of the effects of innovations on the workers. We will find that, while some innovations do decrease worker skill, several of them have increased worker autonomy and skill, and that overall, SuperStores, as an organization, has emphasized workers' autonomy and skill rather than management control and routinization of the work.

In addition to the question of environmental uncertainty, several authors (particularly economists) have focused on the question of environmental munificence. If the change in the environment leads to a performance gap, firms are likely to try to innovate to return to a state of satisfactory performance (March and Simon 1958). Large firms are more likely to have the slack resources available to allow innovations to survive an initial period of market hostility (Schumpeter 1942). In the retail food industry, Levin, Levin, and Meisel (1985) found that the spread of the grocery scanner was determined by such market factors as average store size, concentration, and growth rate. They find that firms in markets with larger stores, lower market concentration, and rapid growth were the ones most likely to adopt the innovation first. Thus, it not simply the heterogeneity of the environment that is crucial but also the munificence of that environment. If the environment is complex but quite munificent (the Garden of Eden is one example), then organizations do not need to innovate to achieve satisfactory performance. However, in the face of a complicated and competitive environment, firms do need to innovate to maintain a satisfactory level of performance. Large firms are more likely to have the resources to introduce innovations in a tight market.

Politics

Finally, there are those who argue that innovations in work organizations result from a political process. Bacharach and Lawler (1980) and Pfeffer (1981), for example, view organizations as shifting coalitions of interest groups that attempt to modify the organization to suit their local needs. Each group's power is in part determined by its position in the organizational structure (Hickson et al. 1971, Pfeffer and Salancik 1978). The decision to change structure can also be based on a "strategic choice" by the "dominant coalition" (Child

1972). For example, Stone (1974) argues that the implementation of a detailed division of labor and internal labor market in the steel industry was an attempt by owners to divide, and thereby better control, the militant labor force. Pettigrew (1972) notes the interaction between information processing and power. He argues that gatekeepers, who control the flow of information, are in a strong position to influence organizational innovations in ways that favor the gatekeeper's interests.

While each of the above perspectives is helpful in understanding organizational innovation, they are all limited. In this book, I will develop an integrated theory of organizational innovation that incorporates the insights from each of these perspectives. This theory, which I call the politicized context model, combines environmental, technological, and political factors to explain the course of innovations in organizations. I will follow Hickson et al. (1971) and view power as a property of the relationship and not of the actors in that relationship. As Hickson et al. note, when organizations are conceived as systems of interrelated departments, the division of labor becomes the locus of power (1971:217). By focusing on the division of labor and the subunit's relations with other units and with the environment, we can better understand the power component of organizational innovation.

The Politicized Context Model of Innovation

Building on the models cited above, I have developed a model of innovation that includes technological, environmental, and political factors. I use this model throughout the book to analyze the various innovations in the retail food industry. I show how the final form of each of these innovations was the result of a combination of market and social factors.

Figure 1.3 gives the model for a politicized context theory of inno-

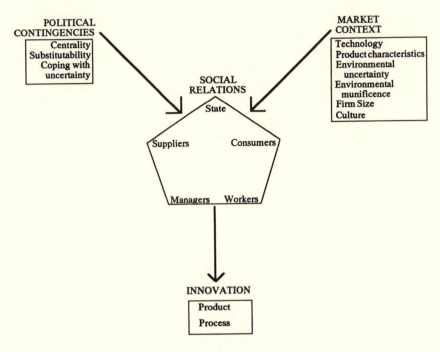

Figure 1.3. A Politicized Context Model of Innovation

vation. Following the environmental perspective, context variables—the nature of the product, uncertainty, munificence, firm size—determine innovation outcomes, either a process or a product change. I incorporate technology into the model as a context variable, because technological change is part of the environmental change that firms must negotiate. I also include culture as a context variable, largely because of its influence on demand. As illustrated by the model, the relationship between environment and innovation is not a direct one. Changes in these context variables (in particular, a new invention) change the social relations of the system, that is, the relations between the firm's managers, the workers, the consumers, the suppliers, and the state. Political contingencies—such as coping with uncertainty, substitutability, and centrality—determine the relative influence of each of the actors over the form of the innovation. The innovation is a new set of social relations. This model of innovation is similar to Child's (1985) model of the factors that influence various types of management strategy. His model, which focuses on the worker-management relation and the effects of management strategies on such worker attributes as skill and control, includes labor and product markets, organizational characteristics, task characteristics, institutional environment, and organizational culture.

The following section elaborates on the development of this model. I then use the model shown in Figure 1.3 to analyze the implementation of various innovations in the supermarket industry. We will see that the outcome (an innovative set of social relations) is the result of market and political factors, as well as cooperation among the actors.

Market Context

As the discussion of the deskilling thesis argues, technical advances are an important component of organizational innovation. A variety of case studies (Glenn and Feldberg 1982, Kraft 1979, Whalley 1984, Zuboff 1988) have shown support for this deskilling thesis, finding over time in various industries that work has been transformed by an increasingly fine division of labor and mechanization of production. All of these authors argue that the history of organizational innovation is in part technologically driven, with new machines introduced into the labor process to transfer control from workers to managers. These theories imply that the process of implementing new technology is relatively straightforward, limited only by the pace of progress in science and engineering and by management's desire to control the work force.

There has been a variety of criticisms of the deskilling thesis. Many of them revolve around the fact that Braverman and others have underestimated the ability of workers to resist this encroachment into their domain. Penn (1982), for example, argues that if workers can monopolize control over the production process before deskilling innovations (in this case, mechanization) are introduced, they are often able to maintain their monopoly over the work even after the introduction of the new technology. Noble (1979), discussing the case of numerically controlled machine tools in Norway, notes that knowledge of new inventions helps workers and their unions bargain for more favorable conditions for implementing technological innovations. Finlay (1988), based on his study of longshore workers, claims that management is willing to trade control over the work for increased work speed.

The deskilling thesis also makes some assumptions about the organization of work that suggest how the theory might be limited. For example, several authors have argued that there are important limits to management's ability to specify the microdetails of the production process (Halle 1984, Juravich 1985, Kusterer 1978, Sabel 1982, Shaiken 1984). These researchers argue that successful production depends on worker cooperation to fill the interstices in management's plans. In fact, Halle's (1984) description of the ability of workers in a chemical plant to analyze and to modify the automated production system to suit their own needs, which sometimes did and sometimes did not match the stated goals of the firm, casts doubts on Zuboff's assertions about workers' inability to function in the realm of abstract reasoning created by automation and the workers' lack of power in the face of this new tool of management.

In addition to this power component, there are flaws in the deskilling argument that grow out of its underspecification of the organizational implications of the thesis. Attewell (1987) claims that the division of labor is self-limiting because finer divisions of work increase the cost of passing work from one worker to the next. Also, the deskilling thesis assumes an ever-increasing amount of knowledge on the part of management. The cost of collecting, processing, and acting on that growing body of knowledge can become quite burdensome, particularly in the face of high variability in the production process. For example, as firm size increases and, more importantly, as firms become more diversified, it becomes more difficult to centralize decision making and to develop bureaucratic rules that will adequately deal with the contingencies of every part of the firm (Williamson 1985, ch. 11).

Downs and Mohr (1976) suggest that the outcome of an adoption decision is the result of the interaction between the various organizational characteristics and the characteristics of the innovation. This suggests that technology is important, but its impact is influenced by the context in which it is embedded. As discussed in the section on environment, that context includes the firm size, the amount of competition, and the amount of uncertainty in the environment. As Fligstein and Dauber (1989) note in their review of the literature on organizational innovation, there are several, competing theories of the process by which firms adopt innovations. For example, while neoclassical economists, including contingency theorists and transaction cost analysts, argue for a tight coupling between the environment and the actions of managers, other theories point out that the relationship is not so direct and that for a variety of reasons, firms may determine whether or not to adopt innovations, using "suboptimal" criteria. For example, as the Carnegie School theories of March, Simon, and Cyert note, organizations develop routines, and they will continue to follow those routines, even in the face of environmental change, unless these routines become obviously impractical (Cyert and March 1963, March and Simon 1958). Even then, they will tend to make incremental changes until they find a course that will suffice, rather than searching for the major changes that might maximize. It is not that members of management are stubborn, but rather, given the limits on rationality, that they are not able to make the calculations that would specify the link between environmental changes and performance and also allow them to discern the maximizing strategy. In addition, the institutional theorists suggest that firms adopt innovations that they perceive will confer upon them legitimate status in their interorganizational environment, although these changes may not be the ones that maximize performance (Meyer and Rowan 1977, DiMaggio and Powell 1983). Meyer and Zucker (1989) note that by exploiting powerful institutional resources firms can "permanently fail" at other performance criteria. These theories suggest that, while firms may be under pressure to adapt to changes in their environment, they may not yield to those pressures. They also suggest that firms have to respond to the institutional (cultural) as well as the market environment.

The Web of Social Relations

Changes in the environmental factors in the model upset the relations among the actors in the organization. One of the contributions of the politicized context model is that it explicitly specifies the variety of actors in the social system. It also points out that each of those actors is a political entity, with interests and political resources available to defend those interests. The following section elaborates on the inclusion of the various actors in the web of social relations.

Much of the literature on the politics of innovation has focused on the worker-manager relationship (Braverman 1974, Edwards 1979, Wilkinson 1983, Wood 1982, Zimbalist 1979). These theorists have noted that technological innovation is often a medium for the struggle between the interests of the workers and those of capital. Jones (1982) notes that the effect of numerically controlled machine tools on worker skill depends on union strength and the specific organization of work as well as on contextual factors such as product demand and type of technology used. Sorge and Streeck (1988) argue that innovations are the result of strategic choices by management and workers, choices made with an eye to product markets and labor markets. Thus the web of social relations in Figure 1.3 includes both workers and managers.

In addition to the worker-manager relationship, several theorists have noted that organizations are open systems and that any theory of organizations should include the relationship between the organization and its environment (Pfeffer and Salancik 1978, Scott 1987, Thompson 1967). The organization's environment includes extra-organizational interest groups that can form coalitions with organizational actors to influence the form of innovation (Selznick 1953).

The *supplier* of the innovation is one such external actor. For example, in a study of suppliers to the food-processing industry, Ettlie (1983) found that the success of an innovation depended in part on whether or not top management from the supplying firm was in contact with customers to encourage the innovation. By going on sales calls or making follow-up visits after the innovation is installed, top management can signal the firm's commitment to the innovation. Firms are less reluctant to innovate if the supplier of the new technology is willing to commit substantial resources to helping implement the innovation. Ettlie also notes that supplier commitment to the innovation facilitates modifying the product to fit customer needs (see the example of boxed beef in Chapter 3).

In addition, the *consumer* of the product is an important actor.

Noble (1984), for example, describes the adoption of numerically controlled machine tools in the United States, as opposed to record-playback tools, as being the result of demand by the U.S. Air Force for parts that could only be machined by numerically controlled tools. Abernathy (1978) and Rubenstein and Ettlie (1979) found that in the auto industry supplier and customer cooperation is important to the ultimate success of incorporating innovations. Glazer (1984) notes that the change to self-service in retailing required that consumers become accustomed to the "work transfer" such an innovation involved. Thus, Figure 1.3 also includes suppliers and consumers into the web of social relations.

Finally, while some of the bargaining goes on within or between organizations, some coalition bargaining takes place in public arenas, such as governing bodies (Selznick 1953). Thomas (1987) notes that technological change is the result of a combination of new inventions, supply of labor and demand for product, and political factors. For example, changes in agricultural production resulted in part from changes in immigration laws and increased union strength at the job site and in Washington, D.C. Similarly, Noble (1979) claims that machinists in Norway have succeeded in controlling the introduction of new technology (numerically controlled machines) and thus in preventing deskilling in part because the Social Democratic government supports worker participation and often worker retraining. Also, by setting standards or regulatory requirements, the state can tilt the playing field in favor of a particular innovation (Cohen and Levin 1990). Fligstein (1985) notes that the spread of the multidivisional form was indirectly the result of government antitrust policy. Therefore, to complete the web, the politicized context model includes the state as one of the actors.

Thus, actors can use their power in different arenas in their attempts to influence the form of an innovation. Corporate campaigns by unions are an example of taking advantage of the open-systems nature of organizations to alter the relations in the system (Raskin 1986). Because of the often higher costs and greater uncertainty of introducing new actors into the bargaining relationship, we would expect that actors would only form coalitions or take the negotiations into new arenas when they fail, or expect to fail, in directly influencing the relationship.

Political Contingencies

If the form of an innovation is the result of a power conflict, how do we determine which actors have how much power? Hickson et al. (1971), building on Emerson (1962), developed a strategic contingencies theory of intraorganizational power. They claim that a subunit's power in an organization is the result of control over strategic contingencies, which are negatively related to the substitutability of the unit's activities and which are positively related to the centrality of the unit to the goals of the organization, the amount of uncertainty, and the unit's effectiveness in coping with those uncertainties (cf. Pfeffer and Salancik 1978). Low substitutability can be the result either of the skill required to perform the positions in the unit, of the rarity of the actors possessing that skill or other factor, or of the large number of positions acting in concert in the unit (for example, when the unit is unionized). Low substitutability can also be the result of the integration required within the unit (cf. Hobsbawm 1964). Subunits are able to use this power to influence outcomes. Also, certain outcomes (for example, a technological change that routinizes one of the sources of uncertainty) can change the balance of power (Burkhardt and Brass 1990, Shaiken 1984, ch. 7). Hickson et al. (1971) theorized about intraorganizational conflict, but we can generalize their theory to include the open-systems nature of organizations. For example, firms in concentrated markets will be better able to introduce innovations that affect their customers because there will be fewer substitutes available (Baldwin and Scott 1987, Levin et al. 1985). Pettigrew (1972), looking at network centrality rather than task centrality, found that having a central position in the information flow gave the gatekeeper position substantial influence over decisions that had formally been outside its domain. These theorists suggest that power is the result of the ability to interfere with or to manipulate the flow of goods or information in the organization. As noted in Figure 1.3, this power is the result of network location (centrality), the skill of positions (coping with uncertainty), or the number of alternatives available (substitutability).

Hirschman (1970) notes that discontented actors (customers or citizens, for example) can use their power in two ways. They can sever the relationship (exit) or they can attempt to modify the relationship (voice). Other actors in the network of relations (managers or government officials, for example) may then, under certain circumstances, modify their behavior to accommodate this action by the first set of actors. Hirschman notes that, in certain circumstances, the threat of exit (which is a special form of voice) is a powerful mechanism in itself. Freeman and Medoff (1984) extend this analysis to the case of workers, unions, and firms. They note that employees can individually make the choice to exit or to voice their concerns but that either action will likely have little impact on the employer. However, by unionizing, employees are better able to affect a situation, both because their collective voice carries more weight (for the reasons noted above) and because the union serves as an institution for distilling various opinions into a common opinion that the majority of workers support.

Hirschman (1970) also argues that the conditions for severing a relationship are not the same as those for forming one. Williamson (1985) notes that there are economies in transaction costs that make it more difficult to sever existing relations. Stinchcombe (1990) also notes that severing existing relationships involves a variety of costs that are not present in creating new ones. Because of the differential costs of severing and creating relationships (given the same price and quality and the same preference functions), the same actor will in one case not enter a relationship and, in another, similar, case, not sever it.

Previous research suggests that innovations in organizations can best be understood using the politicized context model of Figure 1.3. This model implies the following process. A change in the market context, for example, the invention of a new technology or a change in demand, will upset the existing web of social relations between workers and managers and their customers and suppliers, and, possibly, the state. The organization will attempt to adapt to the new conditions by modifying the web of relations. However, the actors in the web will use their political resources, based on their centrality, coping with uncertainty, and substitutability, to modify the web in ways consistent with their interests. The result is an innovation—a new set of relations that fit with the new market context. In this analysis, the modified web of relations, not the new technology, is the innovation. While a new technology may prompt a modification of the social relations, a new invention is not an innovation until it has been incorporated into a viable set of social relations.

Not all innovations lead to political mobilizations. Daniel (1987), for example, found that workers were exposed to frequent changes in technology and organization and, for the most part, did not resist at all. Whether a group mobilizes depends in part on the extent to which its interests are threatened by the innovation (Bacharach and Lawler 1980). For example, once an organization has adopted a certain standard for computer systems, adopting a new system that is technically superior but not compatible can result in enormous costs, such that the perceived benefits of the advanced system (more flexibility, greater capacity, faster processing) are not worth the costs (lost data or data transferring costs, retraining costs, costs of replacing auxiliary equipment, such as printers or terminals, that might be made obsolete). Such a change is likely to be resisted by those using the product (Stinchcombe 1990). In addition to technical problems, there are problems resulting from the loss of status or rewards that the new system may cause. For example, Maltz et al. (1991) found that the implementation of microcomputer-based systems in a large police department was resisted by the data processing division at headquarters because such a system would take control over computing power out of the hands of the data systems employees and put it in the hands of field officers. Detectives also resisted the system because it gave crime analysis capabilities, which are part of the detectives' domain, to patrol officers.

This resistance to change also occurs across organizations, when the innovation will shift the distribution of benefits in the system. When a supplier attempts to integrate forward, the producer will often resist the encroachment into his domain. For example, Porter and Livesay (1971) use the illustration of the resistance to Swift's central processing of cattle (driven in part by the invention of refrigerator cars). Butchers, packers, and jobbers in the East all resisted this invention, because it affected the amount of work that would reach them.

We will explore when individuals or groups are moved to act in response to an innovation. First, if the innovation does not affect them, they will be unlikely to act. If the innovation changes the particular tasks involved, those involved are likely to react if they will lose status as a result of the change. They are likely to lose status if the change eliminates or divides the core tasks of the occupation.

Worker Responses to Innovation

We can think of an occupation as a bundle of tasks (Hughes 1984, Strauss 1985). Every occupation has a core of tasks that identify the occupation (Hughes 1984, ch. 28). For doctors it is examining patients (or their proxies, as in pathology), making diagnoses, and prescribing treatments. For teachers it is lecturing and discussion in the classroom and evaluating students. For meatcutters, it is blocking sides and cutting primal cuts into retail cuts (Marshall 1970). All occupations also include some low-status tasks (Hughes 1984, ch. 30). For teachers, they are completing paperwork and disciplining pupils (Becker 1980). For nurses, they are cleaning duties (Hughes 1984, ch. 30). For meatcutters, they are wrapping meat, serving customers, and cleaning the work area (Marshall 1970). Dividing the tasks in a given occupational bundle can take one of two forms, either hierarchical or nonhierarchical. A hierarchical division of labor carves off the low-status tasks of a particular occupation and gives them to a separate, low-status occupation, or to a machine. Eliminating some of the tasks may reduce the technical competence of the workers by decreasing flexibility. But it may also increase the occupation's status because these low-status tasks are no longer associated with the work and because members of the old occupation may now supervise the new workers. In nursing, for example, as the bundle of tasks increased, the tasks were divided hierarchically into a lower set of tasks (various cleaning duties), which were delegated to aids or maids, and a higher set of duties, including supervising the lower-status workers, with a higher status than the former, full-function nurse (Hughes 1984, ch. 30).

The second form of division of labor is nonhierarchical: the distribution of a central group of tasks requiring a similar level of expertise among two or more equal occupations or machines. A nonhierarchical division produces workers with a diminished bundle of tasks and limited knowledge of the relationship among the tasks unless workers rotate among the different occupations. The new occupations often have low status because of the routine nature of the work and the dependence on higher-status occupations such as managers and engineers to organize the work. Replacing craft workers with assembly line workers (as in Braverman's analysis of deskilling) is a nonhierarchical division of labor.

We need to know the form of a division of labor to determine how workers in a particular occupation will respond to the change. Division of labor does not automatically equal deskilling. If the change will eliminate core tasks (a nonhierarchical division of labor), then the workers in an occupation will resist. For example, workers resisted the introduction of numerically controlled machine tools because they eliminated the core of the job of machinists—determining which cuts to apply. If the change affects only a peripheral task, workers are less likely to resist and even likely to embrace the change. For example, skilled workers may favor a hierarchical division of labor because it frees them from some routine or unpleasant tasks. The employers tend to favor such a system because they do not have to pay high wages for work that an unskilled employee is capable of doing. The worker in a low-status occupation may have no voice in this process because its members do not yet exist if a new occupation is being created, or they may have so little power that their opinions are not considered. The introduction of meat wrappers in the retail meat business followed this pattern, with the low-status tasks being wrapping meat and handling customers (see Chapter 3). If the innovation adds new tasks, workers are likely to resist, unless the new tasks are of higher status than their core tasks, in which case they are likely to embrace their upgrading. Examples of low-status tasks are adding paperwork duties for police officers or maintenance of the coffee machine for the office to the secretaries. Examples of high-status tasks being added are doctors specializing in subfields of medicine and adding the tasks that a specialist concentrates on, or adding the task of taping and finishing drywall to the bundle of either carpenters or painters.[1] Figure 1.4 gives a summary of the expected responses by workers to various changes in their bundle of tasks.

Type of Task

	High Status/ Core	Low Status/ Peripheral
Eliminate or Divide Tasks	Resist (e.g., Machinists and Numerically Controlled Machine Tools)	Not Resist/Embrace (e.g., Cutters and Wrappers)
Add Tasks	Not Resist/Embrace (e.g., Painters and Finishing Drywall)	Resist (e.g., Police and Additional Paperwork)

Type of Innovation (row-axis label, left side)

Figure 1.4. Workers' Responses to Innovations in Their Bundle of Tasks

Customer Responses to Innovation

Similarly, the consumers of the product may or may not resist an innovation. The elasticity of demand varies greatly across different products, and price is not always the primary determinant. For example, the United Farm Workers' boycotts against growers varied in success in large part according to consumers' perceptions of the necessity of the product. For grapes, consumers felt they could substitute other fruits, so the boycott was successful and the union got contracts. The demand for lettuce, on the other hand, is highly inelastic, so customers did not boycott the product (Thomas 1987).

If the change is one in the process, consumers are likely not to notice, unless there is a drastic change in price, so they are not likely to mobilize either to promote or to prevent the change. If, on the other hand, it is a product innovation, generally a substantial change in price or improvement in quality is required to convince consumers that the new product is better than the old. This is due in part to conservatism of preferences and in part to the need to incorporate the new product into a system of production. DeVault (1984) notes that it can be quite difficult to introduce innovations into the household production system, particularly new foods. Innovators will often including training for consumers, especially if those consumers are organizations or institutions, as part of the innovation. For example, IBM's success in the mainframe computer market is due in part to product innovations and in part to its well-established means of training purchasers to incorporate the innovation into their system of task bundles.

Choosing among Innovations

I have shown that innovations are complicated processes and that successful innovations depend on many variables. Given the large number of potential innovations, how can we determine which ones are likely to be implemented? From the above, we can expect that managers are likely to adopt the innovations that require minimal reorganization (that is, those that fit in easily with the established structure), that reduce the high cost but routinized components of the system (that is, those that are likely to produce large benefits and little worker resistance), or that their competitors have adopted (DiMaggio and Powell 1983, Fligstein 1985, Meyer and Rowan 1977).

We would expect the innovations easiest to introduce will be of the form of a hierarchical division of labor, as management attempts to mechanize some low-status, repetitive task that consumes large amounts of labor time (cf. Marx 1977). We would also expect innovations that reduce high-cost labor, using a nonhierarchical division of labor (Taylorism), but only when volume is high (cf. Braverman 1974). A corollary is that any previous innovation that increases volume (by expanding the market) will encourage Taylorism. We would expect innovations that take advantage of established routines to move into new products or services (diversification) (cf. Chandler 1962). Such innovations tend not to be resisted by the organization (although organizations being encroached upon will try to resist). They also tend to take advantage of built-in routines, or the by-products of established routines. Finally, we would expect firms to copy the established innovations of leading firms in their industry (isomorphism) (cf. Fligstein 1985).

We will use the case of the development of the supermarket to show which innovations were adopted and if in fact those innovations are one of the three types: mechanization, Taylorism, or diversification. We will not concentrate on the spread of an innovation throughout the industry (because of isomorphism, for example) but rather we will explore how innovations have become adopted by typical firms in the industry.

Supermarket Unions

The grocery industry is a moderately heavily organized industry.[2] In 1987, about a third of the industry was unionized, with a higher rate (about half) for chain stores (*PG* April 1991). About one-fourth of all manufacturing workers were unionized in 1987 (US Census 1991). The major union for grocery stores is the United Food and Commercial Workers (UFCW). The UFCW currently has about 1.3 million members in the United States and Canada. The UFCW was formed in 1979 by a merger of the Retail Clerks International Union (RCIU) and the Amalgamated Meat Cutters and Butcher Workmen of North America.[3]

The Retail Clerks National Protection Association of America was founded as a craft union in 1890. In 1943, the organization name was simplified to the Retail Clerks International Association. In 1977, the members changed the name to Retail Clerks International Union (RCIU). The Amalgamated Meat Cutters was chartered by the American Federation of Labor in 1897. It was also a craft union, with jurisdiction over all the trades that use a knife, including both packinghouse workers and retail meatcutters. The open-shop movement of the 1920s severely reduced membership in both unions and largely eliminated the Amalgamated's presence in the packinghouses. However, both unions grew in the retail sector beginning in the thirties, in large part because of the growth of food chains, which were easier to organize.

From the beginning, there were jurisdictional fights between the rival unions. In general, they agreed that clerks would be members of the RCIU and meatcutters members of the Amalgamated, with separate contracts for each group of workers. However, marginal classifications, such as deli workers, were a constant problem and were settled on a case-by-case basis. Also, firms and workers often preferred to deal with a single union. Because of their overlapping jurisdictions, a merger was seen as a viable solution to their conflict. In addition, the decentralized structure of both unions facilitated merger. In both unions, locals, rather than the national groups, negotiate contracts within their jurisdiction (generally a city). The 1979 merger between the Clerks and the Meat Cutters created a large, industrial union out of the two craft unions. Currently, some stores still have separate contracts with UFCW meatcutters and UFCW clerk locals, but most locals are in the process of consolidating.

Data and Method

Supermarkets are growing and dynamic organizations in the current economy. They are also central to our economy, politics, and culture. Retail food employment is almost six times employment in auto, steel, and machine tools combined.[4] Drastic changes have occurred in the supermarket industry during the last forty years, including several major technological innovations. Throughout the 1960s and into the early 1970s, there was a decline in profitability in the industry, due to slowing population growth and increased costs (Bucklin 1980, Cornell University, various years, PG April 1976). This decline in profitability was one impetus for innovation. An additional reason for focusing on technological change in food retailing is that some of these changes, in particular the introduction of scanners, have already been analyzed using an economic perspective (Bucklin 1980, Levin et al. 1985, Levin et al. 1987). This research will build on those studies to develop a more complete model of innovation.

This study is based on extensive archival and interview data on the history and current nature of the supermarket industry. I reviewed issues of *Progressive Grocer*, a leading trade journal for the industry, from the period 1967–1988. I also examined older issues from the 1950s and 1960s for background information on specific innovations, such as the use of frozen meat. *Progressive Grocer* publishes detailed annual reports on the industry, as well as articles on current trends and practices. These data provide historical documentation of the changes noted, as well as comparative data for generalizing from the supermarket chain I studied in detail. The journal is a particularly useful source of data for this study because it is a leading journal in the industry and written for the industry.[5] Thus, the journal reflects what is important to the industry. In addition, such a source allows me to gain contemporary accounts of the changes noted, which helps to supplement retroactive accounts from my subjects or from books and articles on the industry. I supplemented these data with historical data from the 1960 to 1985 editions of Cornell University's annual *Operating Results of Food Chains,* as well as various reports on the industry from the Bureau of Labor Statistics. I also reviewed 40 years of SuperStores' annual reports for financial data, which I compared to the industry data gathered from reports by *Progressive Grocer* and Cornell. Those annual reports also provided information on changes in firm structure and strategy.

These archival data were supplemented by interviews with firm managers, union leaders, and workers in the supermarket industry. I concentrated my data collection on one firm: a large, multiregional supermarket chain. The firm that I refer to as SuperStores has 1,300 supermarkets in 20 states, employs more than 100,000 people, and has annual sales of over $17 billion, making it one of the 10 largest firms in the industry. I also collected data from a small, local chain. This firm, which consists of 17 grocery warehouse stores in the Midwest, I call HyperSavers.

I conducted interviews with managers at the headquarters of each firm, with regional managers from the larger firm, and with store employees from stores in four different cities in three different states. I also interviewed union officials at the national and local levels. The sample includes respondents from many different roles in the organization, with an emphasis on store-level employees. I conducted a total of 70 interviews averaging approximately 45 minutes each. In the following chapters, I quote extensively from these interviews, as well as from articles in *Progressive Grocer* and other archival sources. Quotes from archival material are noted by citations to the source. Quotes without citations are from interviews I collected.

Fifty-seven of those interviews were with store-level workers.

Table 1.3. Breakdown of Interviews by Department, Sex, Age, and Seniority

Department	N=	Percent		Age		Seniority	
		Male	Female	Range	Median	Range	Median
Front End	15	33%	67%	17–54	25	1–29	5
Grocery[1]	14	71	29	23–45	27	3–26	7
Meat[2]	12	67	33	21–56	43	1–31	6
Deli[3]	9	0	100	20–53	25	1–15	4
Produce[4]	7	57	43	18–59	29	1–27	11
Total	57	47%	53%	17–59	29	1–31	6

[1]Includes nonfoods
[2]Includes seafood
[3]Includes bakery and cheese shop
[4]Includes floral

Table 1.3 gives the breakdowns by department, gender, age, and seniority. The number of respondents per department reflects the size of each department. The sex distribution also reflects the true distribution across departments (see Table 1.4). The overall sample is quite representative of the unionized segment of the industry. For example, the median age and seniority of members of the United Food and Commercial Workers (the union that represents grocery workers) are 36 years and 7 years, respectively (UFCW 1987). In addition, the union is 52% male. For my sample, the median age is 29 and the median seniority is 6 years, with 47% of the sample being men. My sample is somewhat younger than the industry average and women are slightly overrepresented, but the differences are small and should not bias the results. In 1985, 34% of the industry was unionized. Among supermarket chains unionization was 51% (*PG* April 1987). In addition, these data point to an important characteristic about this industry. Median seniority is reasonably high (roughly 6 years). Average tenure for all occupations in 1987 was 6.6 years (US Census 1991). Thus, despite the common characterization of service work of this sort, this is not a casual labor force.

The interviews varied from very unstructured interviews on the general trends in the industry to more structured interviews (still open ended) on the nature of specific jobs, how they have changed

Table 1.4. Sex Distribution by Department (All Employees
for Two Stores)

Department	Female	Male	Total (N=)
Deli	94%	6%	100% (31)
Front end (checkers)	88	12	100 (42)
Seafood	83	17	100 (6)
Meat	36	64	100 (11)
Front end (baggers)	34	66	100 (35)
Produce	31	69	100 (13)
Grocery	9	91	100 (23)
Overall	58%	42%	100 (161)

over time, and how they have been affected by technological innovations. For example, managers and union officials were asked, "What have been the major changes in the supermarket industry during the last 20 years?" They were then probed to elaborate on each change mentioned. Workers were asked, "How has your job changed since you've been here?" They were then probed to elaborate on the changes and also asked specifically about any new equipment that has been added. In addition to information about innovations, these interviews helped me understand the existing set of social relations and how various actors fit into that web. So, for example, I collected detailed information on the various jobs in the store (such as the tasks involved, formal and informal training required, relative skill, relations with other jobs, and special problems of that job). These data are used to understand how an innovation might change the existing web of relations.

Interviews were tape-recorded and then transcribed. I coded the data from the transcripts and the archival sources and entered it into a text data base on a microcomputer, which allowed me to retrieve the original data (either answers to questions or summaries of *PG* articles) by the code words (Becker 1985, Becker, Gordon, and LeBailley 1984). I also created spreadsheet data bases with longitudinal data on such variables as total grocery sales and average store size (from *Progressive Grocer's* annual reports on the industry) and profit ratios (from Cornell's *Operating Results* and SuperStores annual reports). I used these data to develop histories of the innovations. These histories serve as examples of the processes I am trying to demonstrate.

I also made numerous observations of work practices in supermarkets, both formally during my interviewing and informally during my own visits to the grocery store. Because much, though not all, work in supermarkets takes place in public view, I was able to compare the results of my interviews with my observations in the stores, thereby increasing my ability to judge the face validity of my data.

This combination of current interviews and contemporary archival data has the advantage of being well suited for discovering and analyzing process-based theories. Since I was most interested in the development of the innovations (as modified social structures), I used the archival data as the main data source. The interview data served primarily to provide more detail about how the innovations worked in practice, as well as richer descriptions of some of the changes. These data not only allow us to learn the outcome of certain innovations but also how the outcome occurred. In particular, they allow us to compare innovations that succeeded with those that did not (cf. Fligstein and Dauber 1989:93).

The innovations chosen for study were important changes, or had the potential to be important changes, in the industry. I chose innovations to study based on three sources. First, I asked managers and union officials about the most important changes in the industry over the last 20 years. Second, workers were asked, "How has your job changed?" Finally, from the PG data, I noted changes that initiated several articles during the period studied or that were documented in the annual report. For example, one chart in the annual report was the number of scanners currently installed in supermarkets. This set of innovations will allow us to explore the process of innovation, as well as test our hypotheses about the kinds of innovations that workers will resist.

One limit on these data is that they are not a random sample of firms or markets in the industry. There is a fair amount of regional variation in supermarket practice, in part because the market for groceries is a local one. While I observed in different parts of the country (primarily the Midwest, South, and Northeast), I did not observe in every region. However, my archival data were a source of national coverage. Thus, my descriptions of the changes in the industry are based on a varied, but not random, sample of observations on the industry.

One issue in the literature on innovation is how to measure the spread of an innovation. For example, Baldwin and Scott (1987) note the difference between measuring the interfirm spread of an innovation and the intrafirm spread. Similarly, Levin et al. (1985) measure both the number of units in a market adopting the innovation and the percentage of volume accounted for by the innovation. In this study, I do not have the firm- or unit-specific data to measure the spread of an innovation. I am using a more qualitative operationalization of innovation. I examine the transition from the invention of the innovation to the innovation becoming standard practice in the industry. An innovation has become standard practice when the likelihood of any given unit or firm having adopted that innovation becomes high (with "high" being left undefined). An analogous but somewhat different definition might be when almost all new units in the industry are equipped with the innovation (cf. Romeo, 1977).

Outline of the Book

This study will emphasize the importance of understanding the intersection between the labor process and organizational structure. Because work is often embedded in an organizational context, we cannot properly understand the labor process without also understanding its organizational context. For example, we cannot properly understand the effects of a new technology on the workers without knowing the position of the workers in the organization and without knowing the organization's relation to its environment. Similarly, we cannot understand organizational innovations (such as structural changes) without knowing how these changes affect the labor processes that make up the organization. This study is an attempt to integrate these two modes of analysis to show the utility of a combined model for understanding both technological and organizational changes, using the case of innovations in supermarkets over a 40-year period.

I will use the case of retail food to show how environmental changes lead to organizational and technical innovations and how this process is modified by political factors. By doing so, I will accomplish four goals. First, I will elaborate on the developments in one of our major industries, an industry that has undergone substantial reorganization during this century, particularly during the last several decades, and that has previously been underrepresented in the literatures on organizations and on labor process. Second, I will analyze the complex process of organizational and technological change and show how the fact that organizations are open-systems affects innovations of different types. Organizational change is determined not simply by advances in science. However, it is not a random process either. Managers attempt to deal with the contingencies of their environment in ways that are reasonably predictable, given the nature of firms and the expected reactions of the other components of the system, in particular workers and consumers (Abbott 1989). Third, this work will help to integrate the somewhat parallel literatures on organizational theory and labor process. For example, we will be able to see how innovations in supermarkets fit with the contrasting predictions of the deskilling thesis and the decentralization hypothesis. Finally, I will be able to test the hypotheses noted above concerning when workers are likely to resist various types of innovations.

Chapter 2 focuses on the economic and cultural changes in the United States since Word War II. These are the environmental changes that drive the innovations we observe in the retail food industry. These changes include declining profits in the 1960s and 1970s, slower population growth, increase in the number of working women, increased demand for service, a cultural shift away from red meat and toward lighter meats (fish, chicken) and away from canned vegetables toward fresh produce. Chapter 2 also discusses some of the more macrolevel organizational changes, such as increased firm size and increased store size and a shift in marketing strategy from low price to increased service. Chapter 3 describes the innovations in the meat department. This department has the most craftlike division of labor and was the locus for several important innovations, including both mechanization and Taylorism. Chapter 4 discusses an example of mechanization, the introduction of computers to the store and their effects on work in the front end and in the grocery department. Chapter 5 examines innovations in the grocery and specialty departments, emphasizing the effects of increased store size (diversification) on the work in the department. The chapter will show how this diversification strategy led to a decentralization of the organization. The chapter focuses on the shop-level effects of this decentralization. Chapter 6 concludes the book with a summary of the major innovations in the development of the supermarket and a discussion of what they tell us about the nature of innovations in organizations.

2

ENVIRONMENTAL CHANGES DURING THE POSTWAR PERIOD

CHANGES IN AN organization's environment should lead to changes in the organization's structure. In particular, changes in competitive conditions or changes in consumer preference curves will often motivate organizational or technological changes. These changes can be a result either of economic factors (such as an increase in real income) or cultural factors (changing preferences for red meat versus poultry and fish). This chapter will explore the economic and cultural changes that significantly affected organizations in the retail food industry. I will concentrate on the post–World War II period, with particular emphasis on the period from the mid-1960s to the mid-1980s, a period of rapid change in this industry.

I will show that the major cultural changes during this period—a slowdown in population growth, an increase in the number of working women, and a change in consumer's preference from red meat and canned vegetables toward lighter meats (fish and poultry) and fresh produce—led to a decline in profits in the industry and an increased demand for service. The organizations in the industry responded to these changes by increasing store hours, increasing store size to include more service departments and a larger produce section, and increasing firm size to take advantage of economies of scale. These changes in organizational strategy led to a variety of innovations in the store. Subsequent chapters will detail the history of some of these innovations to determine how consistent they are with our expectations about organizational innovation.

Economic and Cultural Changes

The following sections discuss some of the economic and cultural changes of the last two decades that have had significant impacts on the organization of work in the supermarkets. These changes include declining profits, an increase in the number of working women, and changes in American eating habits.

Profit Squeeze

Throughout the 1960s and into the early 1970s, there was a decline in profitability in the retail food industry. One of the major causes of this decline was the slowdown in population growth. As Table 2.1 shows, after the postwar boom, population growth declined throughout the sixties and seventies. Increasing population provides automatic volume gains for the industry, independent of other factors. However, when the population stabilizes, growth can only come by taking sales from other firms or from selling new products. Firms tried both strategies during this time. The slowdown in population growth led to expansion into new regions and new product lines.

In addition, wages were growing at an accelerating pace (Figure 2.1). From 1966 to 1970, average hourly wages increased at an average of 3% per year. From 1971 to 1975 wages increased at a rate of 8% per year. And, from 1976 to 1980 they increased at a rate of 9% per year (*PG Annual Reports*).[1] Another factor in the profit squeeze was rising energy costs, a major expense at a grocery store. In a typical store, energy costs account for about 1% of sales, about the same as rents or net profit. The combination of increasing wage and energy costs and the slowdown in population growth led to a reduction in profits in the industry. From 1965 to 1975 return on stockholder equity (after taxes) in the retail food industry decreased from 13.1% to 11.7%. During this same period, Standard and Poor's survey of 425 industrials showed an increase in return on equity from 12.6% to 14.2% (*PG* April 1976). Figure 2.2 shows the net profitability (as a percentage of sales) for a sample of chains, from 1959 to 1984. The

Table 2.1. Population, Urbanization, and Average Grocery Store Sales, 1940–1990

Year	Population (x000)	%Change	%Urban	Yearly Sales per Store(real$)	%Change
1940	131,670	——	57%	$ 57,300	——
1950	151,326	15%	64%	90,000	58%
1960	179,323	19%	70%	225,900	149%
1970	203,212	13%	73%	369,400	64%
1980	226,546	11%	74%	519,000	40%
1990	248,710	10%	NA	649,000	25%

Source: US Census, 1985 and 1991; *PG Annual Reports*, various years.

chart shows a consistent downward trend until 1972, when the trend starts rising again. Figure 2.3 shows the same figures for SuperStores. SuperStores was following the industry trend, although somewhat lagged, with its profits hitting bottom in 1975.

The decline in profits was one impetus for the introduction of various technological and organizational changes that would increase the rate of return, either by increasing labor productivity or by increasing the markup (gross profit margin) on items sold. Wallace

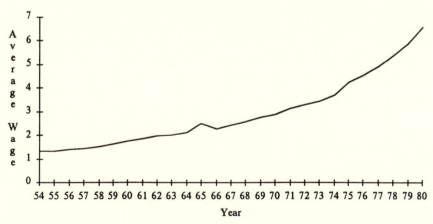

Figure 2.1. Average Wages (Current Dollars per Hour) in the Grocery Industry, 1954–1980
Source: *PG, Annual Reports*, various years.

Figure 2.2. Net Profit as a Percentage of Sales, Supermarket Industry, 1959–1984
Source: Cornell University, *Operating Results of Food Chains*, various years.

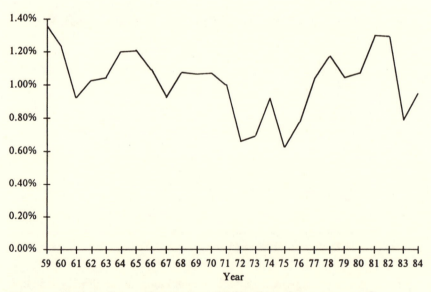

Figure 2.3. Net Profit as a Percentage of Sales, SuperStores, 1959–1984
Source: SuperStores, *Annual Reports*, various years.

and Kalleberg (1982) discuss a similar cause of technological change in the printing industry. March and Simon (1958) argue that such a performance gap is an important prerequisite for convincing a firm to introduce innovations.

Increase in the Number of Women Working

There was also an increase in the number of women working during this time (see Table 2.2). By 1985, over half of all women were in the labor force. In addition, over half of all married women worked. Because of this increase, the demand for service in supermarkets also grew. Working women had less time to shop and, more importantly, less time to cook.[2] In addition, two-earner families had more disposable income, so the cost of convenience foods and service departments was more affordable.

Households were more willing to substitute the paid labor of supermarket employees for unpaid household labor. For example, a 1985 survey of newspaper food editors found that of the top 40 complaints they received about grocery stores, half concerned prob-

Table 2.2. Female Labor Force Participation Rates, by Marital Status

Year	All Women	Married (Spouse Present)
1940	27%	15%
1944	35	22
1950	31	24
1955	34	28
1960	38	32
1965	39	35
1970	43	41
1975	46	44
1980	52	50
1985	55	54
1989	57	58

Source: US Census 1985, 1991.

lems with service, including the top two: long lines at the checkout and uninformed employees in the perishables departments (*PG* January 1986b). Since I do not have comparable information for the 1950s or 1960s, I cannot determine if the demand for service has in fact increased since then. The survey does show that customer service has become important, and the recent emphasis on customer service in the industry indicates that either the demand has in fact increased or that grocery firms have been unaware of, or have ignored, this demand until recently.[3]

Changing Eating Habits

A final cultural change has been the change in eating habits in the United States. There has been a move away from red meat and toward lighter meats (fish, chicken) and a move away from canned vegetables toward fresh produce (*PG* December 1983, *PG* February 1980). These changes in eating habits reflect current trends in opinion about the relationships between diet and health: fresh produce and light meats are perceived as healthier and are therefore in greater demand (Mendelson 1991). These changes put pressure on the firms to reorganize their product mix to accommodate these new tastes. For example, firms greatly expanded their produce sections. In addition, many added salad bars, which catered to both the demand for produce and the demand for service. Salad bars, with a markup of about 70%, also helped reduce the profit squeeze.

Organizational Responses to Industry Changes

There have been several changes in firms and stores as a response to the new technologies and increased demand for service. These environmental changes have led to changes in strategy, which in turn have led to changes in the organizational structure of the firm (including changes in the division of labor in the stores). The new strategies adopted by leading firms such as SuperStores included an increased emphasis on service, an increase in chain size, and a diversification of product lines (and a related increase in store size). These strategic changes have led to a change to a more decentralized structure as management tasks were diffused to store-level employees. All of these changes had important effects on the nature of work in the stores, and I will elaborate on these effects in the subsequent chapters.

Increased Customer Service

Whether the increase in demand for service was real or just recently perceived, there has been a change in strategy by the firms in the industry in response to this demand. The increase in store size facilitates this change in marketing strategy by providing the floor space and volume necessary for increased customer service. Most new departments in the stores (see Figure 1.2) are service departments (delis, bakeries, seafood shops). Even the warehouse stores such as HyperSavers have introduced service departments (*PG* February 1985), reversing a trend toward self-service that started around 1920 (see Glazer 1984, Zimmerman 1955). While much of the store is still self-service, there has been an increase in the number of occupations that are in direct contact with the customer. The following two quotes by store managers illustrate the point:

Q: What do you see as the challenges and opportunities in 1985 for your store and this industry?

Store Manager, conventional store: I've seen a growth in customer sales during the past two years and, along with that growth, I have seen an increase in competition. The competition has not been one of price. I think we have seen the last of the so-called "wholesale price" because basically everybody has it. Three years ago, all you heard was price. Today, we have gone back to the basics of cleanliness and service, and we have boosted our friendly image towards our customers. The challenge of today is converting the price image back to the service image. We will still have to stay competitive—and price will always be part of that—but we will have to treat our challenge as an opportunity to develop long lasting relationships with our customers. (*PG* January 1985)

Store Manager, warehouse store: I see the challenge for us, as a warehouse supermarket, is to change our mix to put profit back into the picture. . . .

We need to expand our fresh fish and frozen fish programs. These are great opportunities. To tackle these opportunities in a warehouse operation, you have to change your merchandising philosophies. We have created the price image, but you have to do more than that today. We've been taking advantage of opportunities to bag groceries and to offer carry out service. . . . It used to be that the standard supermarkets felt they had to compete with the warehouse operations. I think a warehouse manager will have his head in the sand in 1985 if he doesn't see the competitive challenges and the opportunities to be found though increasing warehouse service. (*PG* January 1985)

These two quotes show the change in strategy toward one emphasizing customer service and deemphasizing price competition. The warehouse store manager notes the need to "put profit back into the picture," an allusion to the profit squeeze. The example from the warehouse chain is particularly informative. The warehouse format grew in the 1970s as an attempt to overcome the profit squeeze by eliminating service (for example, requiring customers to bag their own groceries), lowering margins, and raising volume. Such a strategy was no longer viable by 1985, given recent changes in the cultural environment.

Longer Hours One example of this change in strategy is the increase in store hours: staying open later and on Sundays. Table 2.3 shows the increase in store hours from 1975 to 1990. The median number of hours open per week has increased from 82 to 108. The percentage of stores open on Sunday increased from 49% in 1975 to 96% in 1990. And the percentage of stores open 24 hours at least one day per week increased from 7% in 1975 to 28% in 1990. The move toward 24-hour stores is similar to the move toward convenience stores selling gas. If the firm has to have staff available, the additional costs of offering self-serve gas or staying open 24 hours are minimal, so it might be very efficient to do so. For example, convenience stores can sell gas for a price that is the same as or lower than gas stations, since the items in the store have already absorbed most of the overhead. The only additional cost is the pumps and tanks. Similarly, most grocery stores can stay open 24 hours, since they already have stockers working overnight and the added costs of a checker are minimal. Therefore, stores can fulfill the demand for convenient hours with

Table 2.3. Median Hours Open per Week and Percentage
Open Sundays for Supermarkets, 1975–1990

Year	Hours Open	Percent Open Sunday	Percentage 24 Hour*
1975	82	49%	7%
1977	82	60	7
1979	85	71	4
1981	91	83	7
1983	97	94	18
1985	100	96	19
1990	108	96	28

Source: *PG, Annual Reports,* various years.
*At least one day per week.

relatively little increase in costs. As store hours expanded, these new hours became some of the busiest (*PG* April 1976).

This innovation is consistent with our hypothesis that firms will expand into the areas where they already have established routines. The expansion in store hours requires only continuing to do what the firms already do, but for more hours in a week. The impetus was a change in the competitive environment (the opening of convenience stores, which is discussed below) and a cultural change (women working), which increased the demand for longer hours. This innovation created a problem by upsetting labor relations in the industry. Who will work the extra hours the stores are open? Working nights and Sundays is not part of the clerk's traditional bundle of tasks.

The increased hours put the union in a bind. Unions in retail trade were originally formed to reduce long work days (Harrington 1962). The premiums on wages for night shifts and Sundays were designed to discourage long hours. However, consumer demand for extended hours was quite high. For example, this demand for late-night shopping fueled the growth of convenience stores, which were primarily nonunion and which used longer hours as their main selling point (see Table 2.4). Convenience store sales increased from 1% of total grocery sales in 1965 to over 7% in 1990. Extending grocery store hours increased the demand for clerks and also helped the grocery stores compete with the convenience stores. In addition, many union

Table 2.4. Convenience Stores Sales and Stores as a Percentage of Total
Grocery Sales and Stores, 1965–1990

	Sales ($Billion)			Number (Thousands)		
1965	$ 0.7	$ 64.9	1.1%	5.0	227.1	2.2%
1970	2.6	88.4	3.0	13.3	208.3	6.4
1975	6.2	143.3	4.3	25.0	191.8	13.0
1980	12.4	220.8	5.6	35.8	167.1	21.4
1985	20.4	292.2	7.0	45.4	154.0	29.5
1990	26.9	368.5	7.3	56.0	145.0	38.6

Source: *PG, Annual Reports,* various years.

workers were willing to work premium hours to get the higher pay.
The president of the Retail Clerks Union described the union's
dilemma: "We've been working for years to reduce the long tough
grind of extra hours. But now with all this inflation a lot of people
want the overtime. . . . The trend toward longer store hours means
more manpower needs—a chance for some of our weaker locals to
build their membership strength. Also, the more big retail chains stay
open, the more they cut into the convenience stores and
mom'n'pops. This may help membership in the long run as well"
(*PG* January 1975:81).

Because the convenience stores were largely nonunion, the union
had a strong interest in keeping the unionized chains competitive.
The Clerks Union did not oppose extended hours, so long as workers
were paid a premium, and senior workers had the right to work the
premium hours, as well as the right to refuse those hours if they
wished. For example, from 1971 to 1983, for clerks at SuperStores the
premium was 25¢ per hour for work after 6 P.M. and double time on
Sundays. In 1983, the union and SuperStores agreed to lowering the
Sunday premium to time and a half. This change reflects the change
in attitude toward weekend work, a result that is consistent with our
expectation that workers will not resist changes that add to their core
tasks, in this case, increasing the demand for clerks.

Thus, there was a strong demand for longer hours. In addition to
the pull factor of more women wanting to shop at night and on
weekends, there was also the push factor of increased competition
from convenience stores, whose main competitive advantage was

longer hours. Companies wanted to fulfill this new demand because the added costs, except for labor, were low. Fixed costs actually decreased because they were spread over more hours. Since sales during these times were high, particularly on Sundays, stores' volume of business was great enough to cover the premium pay, if the premium was not too large. The change from double time to time and a half represents this change in attitudes on the part of both employers and the union. The premium is now designed as a reward for those who work the less desirable hours, rather than as a means of preventing stores from staying open on Sundays. This is an example of a successful innovation that takes advantage of a new market (evening and weekend shoppers) by diversifying through the use of established routines and that adds core tasks to the worker's bundle. As expected, workers did not fight this change.

Service Departments   Firms also filled the increased demand for service by introducing various service departments into the stores. As the opening comparison between a 1950s store and a 1980s store indicates, many stores now have delis, fish markets, bakeries, restaurants, cheese shops, pharmacies, and video shops, as well as greatly expanded sections for produce and nonfoods–general merchandise, including auto parts, school supplies, cosmetics, small appliances, and electronics. Table 1.2 shows the growth in the number of stores with various service departments. By 1990, 73% of stores had delis, 56% had some sort of in-store bakery, and 33% had fresh seafood shops. These new departments require workers who have competences not previously required of grocery workers because the job was previously part of another organization, such as baker or cook, because the job requires knowledge of new products, such as the expanded produce section or the fish market, or because product demand differed significantly from store to store.

Service departments provided high-margin sales, potentially easing the profit squeeze. Groceries have a markup (gross margin) of 10% to 20%. Service departments have markups ranging from 35% to more than 100% (*PG* February 1976a). Thus, the customer service strategy allowed firms to fill the demand for customer service as well as to increase gross margins. These shops were also in a strong position to compete with independent delis, bakeries, and the like. In their study of the changing work environment of bakers, Steiger and Reskin (1990) document the growth of in-store bakeries. They note that these bakeries tended to be better capitalized and have more modern equipment that independent bakeries. Also, their overhead was lower because much of it was shared with the rest of a very large store. Finally, because of their location in a large grocery, the in-store specialty shops had access to a considerable traffic flow from which to build a clientele.

However, these changes toward a strategy of customer service put a strain on the organizations. For example, firms that sold cooked foods had to devise marketing plans at the store level in order to meet the local demand for table food, which varies by region, class, and ethnicity. At SuperStores, these operating decisions had previously been made at the division level. SuperStores consists of 12 divisions with about 100 stores in each division. Some divisions are quite compact (for example, the Cincinnati division, which is bordered by Columbus, Indianapolis, and Louisville divisions). Others, however, are more dispersed (for example, the Carolinas division, centered in Charlotte, North Carolina, and covering two states). Because of the need to respond to local demand, SuperStores either had to collect detailed information about local demand, process it at the division office, and use this data to create marketing plans for all the stores in the division; or they had to reorganize the authority structure to give more autonomy to the store managers and workers. In fact, they chose the latter course, as we will see in Chapter 5.

Increased Store Size and One-Stop Shopping

Perhaps the most dramatic change in the retail food industry in the last 40 years has been the increase in store size. This increase is not due solely to increases in total population or to increased population concentration but rather to a change in management strategy toward larger, more inclusive stores, rather than numerous, smaller stores. As Table 2.1 shows, there has been a vast increase in average annual sales per store from 1940 to 1990. In 1940, a typical grocery store averaged $57,300 per year in sales (1967 dollars). By 1990, the typical store averaged almost $650,000 dollars per year (1967 dollars). During this same period, population increased gradually, and urbanization leveled off. For example, between 1970 and 1980, sales per store increased by 40%, while population increased only 11%, and urbanization increased by only one percentage point. This increase in store size was fueled not by population pressures but rather by a desire to take advantage of economies of scale and also a change in management strategy toward one-stop shopping, including more and more goods and services within the domain of the supermarket. The increasing suburbanization of the population and the diffusion of the automobile provided the initial impetus for the large, suburban supermarket. Chandler (1962) gives a similar explanation for the growth of retail stores at Sears.

The larger stores are not simply bigger versions of the smaller stores; they do not simply carry more of the same products. Rather, the increase in store size has resulted in increased specialization within the larger departments and an increase in the number of departments. These two factors have led to an increase in the number of occupations in the stores. The typical grocery store in 1973 was 19,500 square feet and had 50 workers (McDonald 1982). By 1980, the typical store was 29,400 square feet with 77 workers, and the newer stores were averaging 45,000 square feet with 131 workers. For SuperStores, average store sales, in real dollars, went from $563,000 per year in 1950 to $3,225,000 by 1980. In current dollars, average supermarket sales across all firms were $8.8 million per store per year in 1990. For chain supermarkets, sales averaged $10.9 million per year. The newer SuperStores stores were averaging $25 million per year, with some of the more successful stores averaging $50 million per year. Thus, this expansion program has led to the creation of stores that are substantial economic entities.

Stores were becoming more labor intensive, in terms of workers per square foot, because the new service departments required more workers, both for in-store production and for direct customer service. The increased store size not only increased the number of occupations in the store but also increased management's problem of overseeing the more diverse activities within a store:

SuperStores Division Manager: I think the biggest change for us has been the size of our stores and of course the responsibilities that go along with the change in size of stores. Not so long ago we would have 10,000-, 15,000-square-foot stores as normal, 15 years ago. Now a 60,000-square-foot store is not out of the realm of possibility at all. There might be 5 employees in a 10,000-square-foot store, compared to 150 to 200 in a 60,000-square-foot store. It's a big change. Our managers might have been the best person stocking groceries 20 years ago. He came up through the ranks in a situation like that. Now, the manager's job is obviously a lot more complex and has a lot more to do with his ability to deal with people, lead, motivate, challenge, and train than it did in the past.

This increased store size has resulted in many changes in worker and management responsibilities. More tasks have been included under one roof, and there has been an increased division of labor (see Figures 1.1 and 1.2). The functions of the grocery store have expanded. The industry calls it one-stop shopping. The idea is to include as many retail goods and services in one location as possible, in order to capture as high a percentage of the total retail dollar as possible. This strategy also reduces the labor of shopping for the customer, which is consistent with the demand created by the increase in the number of women working. There has been a shift in the location of the supermarket in U.S. culture, from a place to buy groceries to the universal store. For an increasing variety of items, the supermarket (with its expanded product lines and expanded hours) is the first place to go to buy a given item. Firms have diversified by expanding on existing routines (including the routines of their shoppers). Once a firm has set up the routines to sell a variety of goods, it is a natural progression to expand into selling a greater volume of the same items and a greater variety of those items. However, the innovation was not unproblematic.

As store size increased and the number of stores decreased, stores had to serve a wider range of customers since they were drawing from a wider geographic area (everyone who drove past the store on their way home from work instead of those who could easily walk to the store). This was one impetus for the expansion of lines of products, since different customers have different buying habits. Some of the differences are cultural (whether a customer buys rice, pasta, or potatoes), some are class-based (whether a customer buys sirloin or round steak), and some are just idiosyncratic (whether a customer buys peas, green beans, or broccoli). So, the store had to tailor itself to as wide a variety of customers as possible. This diversification was in part a response to the heterogeneity of the market as store size increased.

In addition, individual supermarkets had limited abilities to grow by specializing and selling to a wider market. Most people shop within a few miles of their home. This precludes a marketing strategy of selling one product to a national (or even citywide) market—a strategy that mail-order retailers have found quite successful. However, by including more and more products (and services) in a given store, supermarkets can expand by selling a greater variety of products to each customer or by attracting an increased variety of customers, thereby taking full advantage of all the potential customers in their area.

Retail firms in addition to supermarkets began expanding during this same period. In *The Big Store*, Katz (1988) describes Sears's attempts to take advantage of a similar one-stop-shopping strategy. In this case, the related lines were financial rather than soft goods and hard goods. Sears's management realized that in addition to their retailing business, one of their main businesses was lending money through their credit cards. They decided to use their facilities, their customer base, and their experience in the financial business of lending money (through their credit cards) and selling insurance (through their Allstate division) as a basis for expanding into real estate (Coldwell Banker) and investment sales (Dean Witter). Again, a firm expands into areas that take advantage of established routines. Sears filled its needs for experienced personnel by acquiring established firms, thereby getting the necessary task bundles from outside.

What the example of the one-stop-shopping strategy in retailing (both food and nonfood) suggests is that as firms innovate, they innovate into areas related to the ones in which they are already established. During the 1960s and 1970s, there were a large number of firms that expanded into areas with which they had little experience. This conglomeration strategy was unsuccessful in most cases (*Economist* 1991). Thus, while firms can grow by moving into new areas, prior experience in a related area may be an important prerequisite for successful innovators. Peters and Waterman (1982) make the same point from their study of successful firms in several industries. They suggest that firms "stick to their knitting." March and Simon (1958) also claim that innovations that build on existing organizational routines should have more success than those that require developing many novel routines—a process that would tax the information-processing capability of the organization.

The change in strategy in response to the economic and cultural changes in the firms' environments put a strain on the old web of relations between managers, workers, and customers. As stores got bigger, the old relations between managers and workers (direct supervision) were no longer sufficient. Also, as stores included more goods and services, firms needed workers with skills not found in the collection of tasks previously included in the store. Finally, as firms integrated the sale of table food into their business, they needed better feedback mechanisms between the stores and the customers. The following chapters analyze the structural changes that the firms introduced to cope with the challenges this one-stop-shopping strategy created.

Increased Firm Size

In addition to increasing the size of the store, more firms have stores in several regions. In the retail food industry firms range in size from a single store to a small number of stores, to local chains, to regional chains, to multiregional chains. As firms move into many regions, regional differences become increasingly important and stores must develop marketing strategies that will match the mix of products to local demand.

There has been tremendous growth by chain stores, both in percentage of the total retail food market and in terms of chain size. Figure 2.4 shows the increased market share of chains, particularly the large chains. From 1948 to 1987, chain stores' market share has increased from 34% to 65% of total grocery store sales. In addition, the largest chains (of more than 100 stores), increased their share from 27% to 45% of the total market. These chains have grown primarily through mergers with existing chains. Ninety percent of the growth of the top 20 firms was due to acquisitions (UFCW 1980). There was a hiatus on acquisitions from the mid-1960s to the

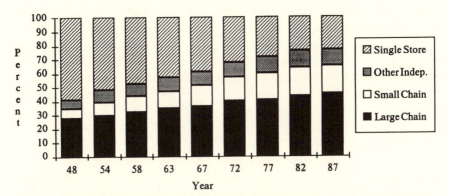

Figure 2.4. Percentage of Total Grocery Store Sales by Firm Size, 1948–1987
Source: US Census, *Census of Retail Trade,* various years.
Note: Single store—Firms with exactly one store.
Other Independent—Firms with 2–10 stores (2–9 stores for 1982 and 1987).
Small Chain—Firms with 11–100 stores (10–99 stores in 1982 and 1987).
Large Chain—Firms with over 100 stores (100 or more stores in 1982 and 1987).

mid-1970s as a result of the Federal Trade Commission's antimerger policy aimed at the big chains (Marion 1979, UFCW 1980). However, after those bans were lifted in the late 1970s, the wave of mergers by the big firms began anew (UFCW 1980). In the same manner that Sears expanded into financial services through mergers, these firms found it easier to expand into new regions by acquiring existing firms, with their already established set of routines, rather than re-creating those routines from scratch.

Firms expanded to increase profits by taking advantage of economies of scale at the wholesale level and by having monopoly power in local markets (Marion 1979, Cotterill 1986). A large firm can spread its advertising costs and warehousing costs over many stores, thereby reducing overhead per store. In addition, advertisers often give discounts to big customers, further reducing per-store costs. A multicity firm can also gain market share, at the expense of short-term profits, by cross-subsidizing the losing division with some of its more profitable divisions where the chain already has a large market share. Marion (1979) found that 6 of 14 large chains operated at least some of their divisions at a loss from 1970 to 1974 and even more of the chains operated at least some of their divisions at a loss for at least one of those years. Finally, diversification reduces a firm's vulnerability to regional economic slumps. It also reduces the firm's dependence on customers or workers in any one region, increasing the firm's power with respect to its workers or its customers.

Summary

There have been several important economic and cultural changes in the last 40 years that have had large impacts on the retail food industry. These include the slowdown in population growth, the increase in the number of women working, and the cultural change toward preferring lighter meats and fresh produce. The industry also faced increased costs, particularly rising wage and energy costs. These changes resulted in declining profits during the late 1960s and early 1970s and in an increased demand for services.

The organizations responded to these changes by diversifying to include more services in their product mix. They also increased firm size and store size to take advantage of economies of scale and to make room for new service departments. To overcome the problems that were created when these larger stores were managed exclusively from their parent offices (the bounded rationality problem), firms decentralized their organizational structure.

The following chapters analyze some of the major innovations that produced the transformation illustrated by the comparison between Figures 1.1 and 1.2. I use the politicized context model to explore these innovations. I will also examine the effects of these innovations on labor processes in the stores.

3

THE DEGRADATION OF WORK?: THE MEATCUTTERS

THIS CHAPTER WILL be the first of three chapters that focus on specific innovations in particular departments of the supermarket. The meat department is an example that illustrates the transformation of a craft occupation as the result of various innovations, including mechanization and Taylorism, both through hierarchical and nonhierarchical divisions of labor (cf. Braverman 1974, Edwards 1979).

After a description of the meat department in the pre–World War II era, the chapter traces the development of the various innovations since that time. We will see how the changes in context for supermarket firms motivated various innovations. This chapter will also emphasize the importance of worker responses to change, applying the politicized context model described in Chapter 1 to the case of the meat department.

Mechanization and the Division of Labor

In 1940, the typical meatcutter worked in a full-service meat counter and cut meat with knives. He served a three-year apprenticeship before becoming a journeyman. His was a very skilled and independent occupation. Major changes and problems occurred when the formerly independent butchers first began working in a grocery store:

> The first meat shop in a grocery store was in 1904, in Kroger's of Cincinnati. Before this time, all meatcutters worked in butcher shops. It was not a smooth transition. In order to control inventory and cash flow, Barney Kroger put cash registers in the meat department. Previously, the meatcutters would make change out of their aprons. The new cash registers were always breaking down for mysterious reasons. So then, Kroger put a female cashier in the department to run the register. The cutters decided that they needed to keep the windows open, even during the winter. So, Kroger built a small room for the cashier, to keep her warm. The cutters then began verbally abusing the cashier with crude language, till she couldn't work there anymore. Kroger responded by hiring a male cashier. The cutters threatened him with physical abuse. (Laycock 1983)

The high status of the meatcutters is reflected in their traditions of independence and manliness (cf. Marshall 1970). They strongly resisted the grocery owner's attempts at supervising their work, including their handling of his money. While the division of labor was largely hierarchical (selling was not part of the cutters' core of tasks), it was the attack on their status, in particular, their autonomy, that meatcutters were resisting. Roethlisberger and Dickson (1939) note that the loss of prestige symbols (such as making change out of their aprons) can have a demoralizing effect on the workers and hence will be resisted, as in the example above.

Once meat cutting became a department in a grocery store, that position consisted of the following bundle of tasks. Cutters would unload hanging sides of meat sent from the packinghouse. They would then "block" the sides, cutting them into smaller, primal cuts (ribs, rounds, loins, etc.), using knives and handsaws—a process referred to as busting. They would then send the meat "down the line." Here cutters would cut and trim these primal cuts into retail cuts (various steaks, roasts, and ground meats), using a variety of knives, slicers, and grinders. They would then put these into the case. Cutters also wrapped and priced the meats the customer ordered and cleaned the cutting room. The meat department at this time was a service meat counter. The cutter had to know not only how to order and cut the meat but also how to handle customers. He had to answer their questions about the quality and preparation of different cuts of meat and also to handle customer complaints. The inclusion of the meat department in the grocery store marked the beginnings of the one-stop-shopping strategy noted in Chapter 2. The meat department was the precursor to the specialty shops of the 1970s and 1980s, such as the delis and seafood shops.

Of the meatcutters' bundle of tasks, the wrapping, cleaning up, and talking with customers was done mostly by apprentices (Marshall 1970:68). Journeymen blocked sides and cut, trimmed, and ground meat. In addition, the journeymen would specialize; some busted sides and others worked "on the line." Marshall claims that the line tasks (cutting primal cuts into retail cuts) are the "central tasks of the job of meatcutter" (1970:36). Apprentices who wished to advance wanted to learn these tasks. Also, "in every store there are some journeymen who cut and saw meat with expertise. They have the respect of their fellow workers and seem to be at the spiritual as well as physical center of the workplace" (1970:70).

In the immediate postwar period all workers in the department were journeymen cutters or their apprentices and used hand tools, knives, and saws. Meat production was craft work and was under craft control. While the firms owned the tools, union rules gave workers monopoly closure over use of the "tools of the trade."

The large increase in population and relative prosperity during the period from World War II to the 1960s led to increased demand for meat. To fulfill this demand, four major changes were introduced in the meat department: power saws, self-service, wrapping machines, and wrappers. These changes were all designed primarily as means of increasing output to meet rising demand.

Power Saws

In the 1950s, power saws were introduced, greatly reducing the amount of time required to cut meat. However, this change did not decrease the technical competence required to determine where to apply the cuts. No one I interviewed said that the introduction of the saws reduced the skills of the cutters. The difference was that now the strength for the cut was provided by a motor rather than by the cutter's muscles. Also, it was still dangerous work, perhaps more dangerous. One cutter put it rather bluntly: "I've had some fingers sewn back on. This is dangerous work. It's not if you'll lose a finger, but when."

Power saws did not standardize the inputs or the products of the production process, nor did they decrease the chances or costs of making a mistake (Perrow 1967). In fact, power saws may have increased the costs of making a mistake, as the above quote points out. The introduction of the power saws is an example of a type of technological change that did not reduce the competence required because, while the new technology did increase productivity, it did not standardize the work (cf. Tushman and Anderson 1986).

This new technology did not disrupt the relations of production. Cutters knew where to apply the cuts, and they incorporated the new techniques into their apprenticeship programs, so the skills were reproduced. The technology was fairly stable and well established. The meat saws are simply standard band saws, so there was little need for special relations between suppliers and retailers. This was a process change, so the firms did not need to educate consumers about the change. The benefits were divided between the firm, which got higher productivity, and the cutters, who kept control over the work while the arduous task of sawing meat by hand was eliminated. We would expect that workers would not oppose this type of innovation. It mechanized a core task but kept it in the cutters' domain. None of the cutters I interviewed complained about the saws.

Self-Service

The second major change was the conversion to self-service. Grocery departments first introduced self-service around 1920 (Glazer 1984, Zimmerman 1955). However, self-service in the meat department came much later because of limitations in packaging. Traditional brown paper wrapping did not lend itself to self-service because the customer could not see what was inside (an important consideration for a product as variable as a cut of meat) and because the meat had a very short shelf life in paper. The development of plastics that would seal and that were transparent allowed meat departments to convert to self-service (*PG* MidMay 1980). In addition, the increase in population, the elimination of rationing after World War II and the general prosperity of the fifties and early sixties put pressure on the meat department to increase output. Thus, there was an environmental change that suggests that the organization should have responded to the new contingencies. But the innovation depended on the development of a new technology that would allow the innovation. There was no market for precut meat in brown paper, but there was one for plastic-wrapped meat—an example of the need to coordinate technological and organizational innovations within the social relations of the firm. While firms in the industry had largely adopted the self-service strategy throughout most of the store by World War II, they had been unable to expand this strategy to include the meat department. Because of the characteristics of the product (perishable and variable), because of the technology of production (brown wrapping paper), and because of the nature of demand (consumers will not buy meat they cannot see), this part of the market could not change. The development of a new wrapping technology allowed the reorganization of production and the expansion of the self-service strategy to include meat.

By the mid-1960s, self-service was the rule in the meat department. Cutters filled the cases, and customers chose what they wanted. While most stores still had facilities for customers to make special requests of the cutters, customers typically filled their orders independently. Self-service left the cutters free to spend all their time cutting meat, improving their productivity. But they no longer had to know how to handle customers or how to cook various cuts. Their sales skills had been reduced because they were no longer in constant contact with the customers. There was little resistance to this change on the part of the cutters, since they viewed it as a chance to concentrate on their core activity, cutting, especially since customer service had been a low-status task that had been assigned primarily to apprentices. This was a product innovation, in the sense that the stores primarily sold precut meat rather than meat cut to order. However, the main product, the meat, was basically unchanged. The major change was that now meat came cut in standard sizes (1/2-inch steaks, 1-pound ground beef packages) rather than custom sizes. Some customers may have missed the contact with their butcher; however, for most customers, the time and cost savings of self-service outweighed the need for expert advice and special cuts that full service provided. Thus, pressure to increase productivity, combined with technological innovation (plastic wrap), led to the introduction of self-service, which reduced cutters' customer-service skills. This was a hierarchical division of labor, substituting customer labor for cutter labor (Glazer 1984). As we would expect, cutters did not resist this elimination of a peripheral task; many may have embraced the change. Among my respondents, one of the most frequent answer to the question, "What do you like least about your job?" was "dealing with the customers."

Wrapping Machines

The third change, which followed close behind the implementation of plastic wrap for meats, was the introduction of wrapping machines during the 1950s. Wrapping machines have gone through a variety of improvements, but the basic unit consists of a station for dispensing plastic wrap and encasing the meat; a hot conveyor, which seals the wrap; and a scale, which weighs the meat and prices the package. All systems I observed depend on the worker to identify the cut and to enter a code into the pricing station (either the price per pound, or a lookup code). Some machines automate the initial wrapping; others seal the wrap, weigh, and price the manually wrapped package. The fully automatic machines are not always reliable. The head of one of the local meat unions described the problem: "They found they had problems with the wrapping machine. In the mean time they had a hand wrapping station for the oddball things. They found just using the hand wrapping station and a belt-fed conveyor with a heated belt, they could make product faster than the machine, because the machine broke down a lot. When that machine broke down, all production stopped."

Because of the unreliability of the machines (due in part to the variability of the input), the wrapping station was redesigned to supplement rather than replace wrappers. Workers compensated for imperfections in the machinery (in this case, because of the randomness of shape and weight for various cuts of meat). Even the simpler systems require worker knowledge to keep production going. For example, one wrapper told me that his department would resort to a hand iron to seal the plastic wrap when the heating element in their wrapping machine was broken. While the whole process could be automated, a semiautomated system seemed more stable. Thus, the innovation was redesigned to coordinate with the current division of labor, rather than to replace the workers. By having a machine do the most routinized part (sealing, weighing, and pricing) and leaving the less routine (wrapping and identifying the cut) to the workers, firms had a more stable system.[1]

Meat managers estimated that automatic wrappers and weighers reduced labor time by between 30% and 50% (*PG* February 1979). This change had little effect on skills, because wrapping machines only automated routine, low-status work. However, because the machines tended to break down, they depended on worker knowledge to maintain high productivity. The machines also increased worker knowledge to the extent that they still had to know how to wrap product when the machine broke, and they also had to be able to tend the machine. As Kusterer (1978), Sabel (1982) and Juravich (1985) have noted, operatives become an important part of the production process because they know the idiosyncrasies of their particular machines. Cutters did not resist the change because a peripheral task, wrapping, was mechanized.

Meat Clerks

The fourth major change was the introduction of the meat clerks or wrappers. Previously, all the people in the meat department had been either journeymen cutters or their apprentices. In the 1950s, some firms added the new category of meat wrappers (or meat clerks). Their job was to wrap the meat and fill the case. They also took care of much of the customer service. Cutters still made the special cuts, but wrappers would take the orders and answer questions. In union shops, the wrappers were forbidden any work involving the tools of the trade. Now there was an occupation that mediated between the customers and the cutters. Thus, cutters became further removed from customers and the skills of customer service. When a customer wanted a special cut, he or she would ask the wrapper for the cut. The wrapper would generally ask if the customer had more shopping to do, explaining that the order would be ready when the customer returned. The wrapper would then give the cutters the customer's request (for example, to slice a loin into steaks). The cutter would make the cuts and then give the meat to the wrapper, who would wrap it, price it, and give it to the customer. The change to self-service and the introduction of the wrappers combined to transform the meatcutters from a craft that did both production and service work to a craft that did almost entirely production work.

To emphasize the status difference between cutters and wrappers, the wrappers often worked in a separate room from the cutters. The meat locker and the saws and knives would be in one room, and the wrapping machines and the case would be in another. The two rooms would be connected by a conveyor belt. In addition, most of the cutters (all that I met), were men. Most of the wrappers (though not all), were women. Cutters' wages were quite a bit higher than wrappers' wages. For example, in one union local, journeyman cutters made $12.33 per hour (in 1986), wrappers hired before 1981 made $10.89, and wrappers hired after 1981 made $8.30 (see Table 3.1). This wage disparity further enhanced the difference in status between wrappers and cutters (Homans 1974).

The introduction of wrappers allowed the cutters to spend even more of their time cutting. Although there is some skill in wrapping (primarily identifying various cuts of meat to price them and handling customers), assigning the job to wrappers did not reduce the skill of the cutters (they still knew the different cuts). There was little conflict over this change. The meatcutters welcomed the addition of the wrappers, because it freed them from the low-status work of wrapping. An officer from the meatcutters' union described cutters' attitudes toward the change:

> The journeymen, which was a highly skilled profession, and the only skilled profession in the store, at a point said, "We don't want to do that, it's semiskilled, we don't have to do it." They can, but they said, "Give it to the clerks [wrappers]. Give all those menial jobs to the clerks." Today, they're hurting. Today they are looking for work, and the clerks are doing it. So it really hurt them. I guess when times are good, when you can't see too far down the road what's happening, you say, "I'll get out of a little

Table 3.1. Wage Rates among Unionized Grocery Workers, 1971–1979 (Current Dollars per Hour)

Year	Journeyman Meatcutter	Meat Wrapper	Full time Grocery Clerk	Cutter/ Wrapper Ratio	Cutter/ Clerk Ratio
1971	$4.53	$3.38	$3.73	1.34	1.21
1973	5.27	3.97	4.34	1.33	1.21
1975	6.50	5.06	5.33	1.28	1.22
1977	7.69	NA*	6.42	NA	1.20
1979	9.11	7.61	7.50	1.20	1.21
			Average =	1.29	1.21

Source: US Bureau of Labor Statistics, 1973, 1975, 1976, 1978, and 1981a.
*NA—Not available.

work. I'm skilled. I'm the big boy here. I just do this. I don't want to clean up, or whatever." At one time, he did it all.

Since cutters were glad to be rid of the low-status tasks given to the wrappers, this innovation was reasonably unproblematic. There was no need to reorganize relations with suppliers. There was some change in the relationship with the customers, in that customers now dealt with wrappers instead of directly with the cutters. However, the change to self-service had eliminated most of the contact with customers already, so this change was not traumatic. The major difficulty in the reorganization was working out the status relations between the cutters and the newly created position of wrapper. The organization solved the problem by staffing the wrapper position with low-status workers (primarily women), by paying them less and by restricting their access to the cutting room (where the high-status work took place). Homans (1974) notes that such overlapping statuses within a role set helps to facilitate worker interaction, and, I would add, therefore makes innovation easier.

The period from the mid-1940s to the mid-1960s is characterized by increased demand for meat and technological change to meet this demand. The new machines, saws and wrapping machines, did not reduce cutters' skills. The wrappers did take some of the cutters' work, but only aspects that required little skill. This change was a hierarchical division of labor, similar to the change in nursing described in Chapter 1. As expected, cutters did not resist, and even embraced, these changes, which freed them from routine and laborious tasks in their bundle and let them concentrate on the high-status, high-skill tasks of blocking sides and cutting meat. Except for the change to self-service, none of these innovations changed the product, so customers were not a factor in most of these changes. To the extent that supermarkets with the labor-saving technology had lower prices, customers may have embraced these changes also. In addition, most of these changes involved little interaction between the suppliers and the firms. These innovations did depend on new inventions (power saws, wrapping machines, and a nontoxic, clear plastic wrap). However, unlike some of the innovations that we will discuss below, these inventions could all be introduced into the division of labor with little disruption of current relations in production.

The Development of Centralized Meat Processing

The centralization of meat cutting has been the major innovation of the last few decades in the meat department. Following the politicized context model, I begin by specifying the market context and political contingencies. I then examine two different forms of this innovation (frozen meat and boxed beef) and how each affected the web of relations.

Market Context

The change to self-service meat departments established the preconditions for centralized processing of subprimal and retail cuts of meat. Before self-service was introduced, retail stores bought quarters and sides of beef and blocked them—cut the sides into large blocks of beef and then into primal cuts, such as ribs, rounds, and loins—in the store. Centralization is the process of moving blocking out of the stores and into the processing plants.

Retail firms had an interest in centralizing meat processing because in-store processing of carcasses is expensive and has several inefficiencies, including limited division of labor, limited marketing flexibility, and lower return on by-products (*PG* April 1968). Centralization also allowed stores to devote more of their space to retailing, rather than to back-room processing. Finally, shipping sides of beef was both expensive and wasteful. Approximately 14% of a side of beef is bones and excess fat (*PG* August 1971). Packers also had an interest in centralized processing as a means of integrating forward into a related market (cf. Porter and Livesay 1971).

In addition, during the late 1960s and early 1970s, firms in the supermarket industry faced declining profits and increasing labor costs (see Chapter 2), so retailers had an added incentive to move into central processing. Meatcutters were the highest-paid workers in the store. Throughout the seventies, meatcutters' wages averaged 21% higher than clerks' wages for unionized firms (Table 3.1). Finally, from World War II until about 1970, demand for meat was increasing, both on a per capita basis and absolutely, because of population growth. However, beginning about 1970, there was a decline in demand for red meat (*PG* March 1980). As a result, retailers were under further pressure to cut costs, since there was less slack in the system to cover inefficiencies (Cyert and March 1963).

Centralization, however, was limited by the characteristics of the product. The major technological limit to central processing was that cut meat has a limited shelf life (generally three days for untreated retail cuts) (*PG* April 1968). In addition, customers will resist buying meat that has even the appearance of not being fresh (*PG* April 1972).

Political Contingencies

The major actors in the web of meat processing at the retail level are meat packers, retailers, meatcutters, and customers. Meatcutters have traditionally been very independent and resistant to management intrusion into their domain (Marshall 1970, Meara 1974, Walsh 1989). As Walsh (1989) notes, they have been able to enforce this independence in part because of their skill—their ability to cope with uncertainties in the production process. The cutters were also in a powerful position because of their centrality. The meat department accounts for about 20%–30% of sales in a typical supermarket (*PG*

March 1980). In addition, the meat department is considered to be more central than even these sales figures suggest: it is often called the kingpin of the supermarket (*PG* September 1984). Finally, the cutters were heavily unionized (approximately 45% of retail cutters were unionized in 1976, 65% for chain stores [*PG* April 1987]), which, when combined with their skill, made them difficult to replace. In addition, it made their voice option more potent (Freeman and Medoff 1984). Thus, from a control perspective, retail managers had an incentive to adopt innovations that would give them greater control over the in-store production process (Braverman 1974, Edwards 1979). In particular, innovations that routinized the production process or that substituted packer labor for retail labor would reduce the political power of the cutters with respect to the retail managers.

Both the supplier and the retailer markets for meat are characterized by relatively low market concentration. For example, in 1972, the four-firm concentration ratio for meat packing was 22% (Table 3.2). In addition, concentration had been decreasing since the 1940s. Concentration in retail food is also quite low at the national level. In 1972, the four-firm ratio was 18% (US Census 1976). However, at the local level, concentration in retailing is much higher and was increasing. As buyers, retailers are in a national market so the national figure is appropriate. However, as sellers, retailers are in a local market so the local figure is more relevant. In addition, average store size has increased in retail trade (Table 2.1). Average annual sales per store in 1940 were $57,000 (1967 dollars). By 1980, sales per store averaged $519,000 (1967 dollars).

With respect to customers, retailers were in a relatively weak bargaining position. They had fairly low (although increasing) market shares. Thus, while retailers were central to the household economies, any given retailer was fairly easily substituted for another. There were no coalitions comparable to the meatcutters' union. However, the customers are also fairly diffuse and unorganized. Retailers did not have to worry about concerted action by the customers (at least until the 1970s). Rather, it was the aggregate of individual decisions to exit (or not to enter) that allowed customers to exert their power. The relative power of the customer was also increased because individual stores, and many chains, operate in a local market. Stores cannot increase their sales by selling to a given

Table 3.2. Concentration Ratios in Meat Packing and Retail Food, 1947–1987

Year	Meat Packing[1]	Retail Food[2]	Chain Sales[3]
1947	41	—	—
1948	—	—	27
1954	39	45	29
1958	34	49	32
1963	31	50	35
1966	27	—	—
1967	26	51	36
1970	23	—	—
1972	22	52	40
1976	—	55	—
1977	19	—	41
1978	—	53	—
1981	—	60	—
1982	29	—	43
1987	32	77	45

[1]Percentage of value added by four largest firms in industry. Source: US Census 1977, 1992.

[2]Percentage of sales by four largest firms (averaged across SMSAs). Source: Marion 1979 (except 1978, 1981 and 1987 figures, which are estimated from a sample of 20 MSAs using data from *Progressive Grocer's Market Scope*).

[3]Percentage of sales by chains of 100+ stores. Source: UFCW 1980, US Census 1982, 1987.

niche across the country (as, for example, certain mail-order firms do). Retailers are limited in their ability to find substitutes for their relations with their current customers by the geographically limited market for retail food.

Thus, we would expect that packers and retailers would try to introduce innovations that would centralize and routinize the production of meat, that such innovations would be limited or shaped so that they are consistent with household production requirements, and that cutters would resist such innovations and have some success in limiting or altering the innovation but that their success would be tempered by the fact that the innovations are likely to eliminate the basis for their power (Burkhardt and Brass 1990).

Centralization: Frozen Beef

Central processing of subprimal and retail cuts began with frozen meat. Firms first introduced frozen meat programs in the late 1940s, and many saw them as the wave of the future during the mid-1950s. For example, there were eight feature articles on frozen meat in *Progressive Grocer* between November 1954 and September 1957. The optimism about the qualities of frozen meat continued until the late sixties. Frozen meat had a long shelf life and did not require as much in-store labor. For example, a typical self-service fresh meat department in 1955 might have nine full-time and six part-time employees, with labor costs at 7% of sales (*PG* December 1955). A department that dealt exclusively with frozen meet typically had one part-time employee, with labor costs at .5 to 1.5% (*PG* February 1956). Thus, frozen meat filled one of the desires of retailers, the elimination of costly and troublesome meatcutters. Frozen meat also had the advantage of allowing meat buyers to purchase meat when demand was low and supply high (for example, buying pork in the spring) to get a good price and then freezing and storing the excess until the demand increased (*PG* November 1954). Thus, frozen meat could remove some of the environmental uncertainty that packers and retailers faced. There was a variety of such programs, but the most important for this discussion were those sponsored by the major packers.[2]

Swift, the nation's largest meat packer, instituted one such program. In May 1955, six stores in Detroit, Michigan, including several chains and some large independents, were designated as experimental stores for Swift's prepackaged, frozen meat. They used a technique of wrapping the meat in moisture-proof cellophane, packing it in grease-proof cardboard boxes, and overwrapping it with printed metal foil (*PG* December 1955). This method had the additional advantage of creating a brand identification for the product. This program was a natural extension of Swift's earlier move into central slaughtering (Porter and Livesay 1971). The invention that made the change possible was the development of quick-freezing methods, a fairly diffused innovation that had already become established in other food-processing industries. There was also the problem of

Table 3.3. Production Figures for Frozen Meat, Frozen Food, and All Meat, 1950–1969 (Millions of Pounds)

Year	Frozen Meat*	All Frozen Food	Frozen Meat/ All Frozen Food	All Meat*	Frozen Meat/ All Meat
1950	35	2,972	1.2%	22,075	0.2%
1955	250	7,307	3.4%	28,895	0.9%
1960	310	10,868	2.9%	28,203	1.1%
1965	450	14,144	3.2%	31,502	1.4%
1967	420	16,141	2.6%	35,237	1.2%
1968	430	15,335	2.8%	35,295	1.2%
1969	460	15,857	2.9%	36,217	1.3%

Source: US BLS, 1971:603, 604.
*Not including seafood or poultry

developing packing material that would maintain freshness and resist the cold. There was a variety of solutions to this problem, some more innovative (such as coating the frozen meat in plastic wax) and some, like Swift's, in which the technology was not particularly sophisticated (*PG* November 1954, *PG* December 1955, *PG* February 1956, *PG* July 1957, *PG* September 1957, *PG* May 1958).

After six months, the program's success was still uncertain. Frozen meat sales accounted for about 7% of total meat sales (range 4.7% to 9.6%) across the six stores. Part of consumer resistance was the higher price of the frozen product (from 6.5% to 147.9% higher, depending on the cut).[3] *Progressive Grocer* continued to report on experiments involving the retailing of frozen meat. These experiments generally included extensive advertising campaigns by the retailers to persuade customers of the benefits of frozen meat. However, despite two decades of claims that frozen meat was just around the corner, frozen meat never became established. By 1957, almost a decade after it was first introduced, frozen meat accounted for well under 2% of the red meat market, and most of that was sold to the institutional market (*PG* September 1957). By the late sixties, frozen meat had stabilized at just over 1% of total meat production and just under 3% of total frozen-food production (see Table 3.3). By the early seventies, many chains had eliminated the product entirely, freeing valuable freezer space for faster-moving items. Frozen meat simply was not acceptable to the consumer (*PG* September 1957, *PG* April 1968). In an interview, a corporate officer of a regional chain that developed a wax-coating method for frozen meat describes consumer resistance to the innovation: "You can describe that with one word—reluctance. We had a terrific selling job to do in the beginning. It hasn't been an easy one. However, we have found that once the consumer has tried the new product the repeat business has been wonderful" (*PG* February 1956:74). One factor in consumer resistance was the discoloration that often took place during freezing (*PG* April 1968, *PG* July 1970). Most shoppers prefer to buy fresh meat and freeze it themselves. A consumer survey in 1970 found that while 90% of consumers sometimes freeze beef at home, 78% would refuse to buy frozen meat in the store (*PG* July 1970). Thus, the demand characteristics of the product limited the innovation—consumers did not perceive frozen meat as a functional substitute for fresh meat. In addition, while large home freezers are not a requirement of a frozen meat program, most programs geared much of their marketing toward buyers with home freezers (*PG* November 1954, *PG* December 1955, *PG* July 1957). However, only 18% of all households had freezers at this time (*PG* July 1957, US Census 1971). Perhaps most importantly, frozen meat was a product innovation that required households to reorganize their bundle of tasks in home meal production. The vice president of meat operations cited above explains the change:

Q: Explain how a housewife would handle a wax-protected meat item once she wishes to prepare it for dinner?

V.P. Meat Operations: There are two different ways she would use to prepare this meat. If she needed to cook the meat in a hurry—say guests drop in unexpectedly—she goes to the freezer section of the refrigerator and takes out a package of ground beef patties, for example, and puts it in a pan of cold water for five or ten minutes. She next scores the wax with a knife and unpeels it just like the skin on a banana.

On the other hand, with the method that we recommend and the one she would normally use, she takes the package from the freezer section of her refrigerator the day before she intends to use it, and puts it in the normal temperature section. When she's ready to cook it, she takes it out of the refrigerator, scores the wax with a knife and unpeels it. It's thawed out, has all the bloom, its juices are there and it's very attractive. The meat looks just as if it had been cut within the past fifteen minutes. (*PG* February 1956:76).

These changes in household tasks are minor (many people routinely freeze their meat and thaw it as needed). However, it is a change (one cannot buy meat and cook it immediately). As DeVault (1984) argues, even minor changes can upset the delicate balance of household food production. While such product innovations are possible, they generally must offer the consumer some advantage in either price, quality, or convenience to compensate for the cost of having to reorganize the household production system. While there was debate over these issues, frozen meat did not clearly offer any of these advantages. Thus, one limit on the innovation was that it made unjustified assumptions about the structure of social relations (that consumers had freezers and routinely plan meals around frozen meat).

The above quote also brings out another dimension of the market context—the assumption that household production is done by a full-time, female, unpaid worker (the housewife). It is not clear if this assumption was ever valid. However, as noted in Chapter 2, it is becoming increasingly less valid as we move from the 1950s to the 1990s.

Another reason for the failure of frozen meat is that it demanded a significant and costly reorganization of the retailer's operation. In particular, frozen meat required the addition of substantial freezer facilities, both in the back room for storage and on the floor for display cases. These facilities are costly to buy and costly to maintain (*PG* November 1954, *PG* April 1968). Also, at the processor level (whether in-store or at the packers) firms have to buy expensive freezing equipment, use higher cost packaging materials, and have expensive storage facilities (*PG* November 1954, *PG* September 1957, *PG* April 1968). A corporate officer for one of the large chains summarized the problem:

Corporate V.P.: If frozen meat merchandising expands, it may change entirely our present system of meat distribution, with more storage facilities necessary at the packer level, more use of low temperature trucks and more low temperature storage and display facilities in stores. Also, serious consideration should be given to its effects on in-store packaging and conversion of fresh storage space to frozen storage. . . .

It's a three-way proposition.
Swift has provided the first impetus to a great change in handling meat.
The retailers can provide the merchandising know-how and lay plans to
match its growth.
The customer will make the final decision. (*PG* December 1955:70)

This quote also re-emphasizes the importance of customer resistance, which results because the innovation requires a major reorganization of the routines of the actors, and this reorganization
involves costly equipment for the packers, transporters, wholesalers,
and retailers. Thus, as expected, there is reluctance on the part of
these actors to adopt the innovations. Consumer reluctance about the
product interacted with retailers' reluctance to the process to yield
major resistance. This resistance by the customer took the form of not
buying the product, as the market share data show (in the Swift trial,
sale of frozen meat accounted for only 7% of the total). This resistance
by retailers took the form of not adopting the innovation, or of only
weakly supporting it in experimental trials, as one processor pointed
out: "Of vital concern is apathy at the retail level. Personnel are
reluctant to service the case and for the most part are lax on stock
conditions. The general feeling at the store level in conversation with
the processor is 'This is your baby. It is out of my department'" (*PG*
September 1957:190).

We would expect that one barrier to such an innovation would be
resistance on the part of the meatcutters. However, I found no evidence of it. That is not to say that meatcutters welcomed this intrusion into their domain. However, since frozen meat never became a
major portion of all meat sales, meatcutters may not have seen it as a
serious threat to their interests. Meatcutters did resist other forms of
centralization that were becoming more established. Perhaps if
frozen meat had been more acceptable to retailers and consumers,
meatcutters may have reacted more strongly to the change.

While this was a process innovation involving the centralization
of meat processing, it was also a product innovation. The final product, the meat found in the display case, was transformed. As predicted, consumer reaction was important in this case. Consumer
preferences were such that meat that was not perceived as fresh (in
part because of discoloration) was in low demand. Because the market for retail food is reasonably competitive (there is high sub-

stitutability among firms), consumers could choose to shop at any one of a number of locations at very little cost. In addition, in many locations, consumers could choose fresh meat over frozen in the same store (the two products were directly substitutable). Thus, customers manifested their objection through exit, or not entering. As Hirschman (1970) notes, retail firms in competitive markets tend to be sensitive to exit by their customers. Also, frozen meat was a process innovation that required major additions to the retailers' capital and energy expenses. Because smaller packers were the main proponents of frozen meat programs (Swift is an exception), retailers had many alternative suppliers and could easily find a substitute for a packer that adopted a frozen meat program. Even in the case of Swift, the supplier still provided fresh meat to retailers. Perhaps if Swift had converted entirely to frozen meat, it could have used its market power to increase sales of the product. However, this move would have been very risky, particularly in the face of limited consumer and retailer interest in the product and the availability of other large suppliers. Finally, because of the centrality of retailers (there was no direct link between suppliers and consumers), retailers were able to enforce their preferences. The combination of a competitive context and consumer and retailer resistance prevented frozen meat from becoming standard practice. The final blow to frozen beef may have been the invention of an alternative technology that would allow central processing of meat: boxed beef.

Centralization: Boxed Beef

Even though frozen meat had not been a successful innovation, firms in the industry still had the same incentives to centralize meat processing. In addition, as Figures 2.1 to 2.3 show, during the late 1960s and into the 1970s, profits were declining, while wages were increasing. At the same time, demand for meat was declining. Firms needed an innovation that had the benefits of central processing, but without the disadvantages of frozen meat. Boxed beef provided this alternative.

During the seventies, firms began blocking the sides at central meat-processing plants, either owned by the retail firms as part of their warehousing operations or at independent slaughterhouses, such as Iowa Beef Processors (IBP) or Missouri Beef. These processing plants would make the primal cuts and then put them into vacuum bags and then into boxes of uniform size and approximately uniform weight, about 60 pounds. They would then ship these boxes to stores for cutting into retail cuts.

The technological innovation that made boxed beef possible was the development by the Grace Corporation of a plastic that would seal airtight, was nontoxic, and was strong enough to withstand punctures by the bones in the primal cuts. By allowing a shift in the work from many local retail outlets to a few centralized processing centers, this innovation had the potential to rearrange the relations among meat suppliers, retailers, and workers. Friedland, Barton, and Thomas (1981) note a similar process with the introduction of wrapping machines into lettuce production. The following section will describe the process of creating the social relations of centralized beef production.

There was a strong push for boxed beef from meat packers, particularly IBP, and from wholesalers who bought the boxed beef from the packers and then sold it to retail stores. In 1967 IBP began processing retail cut meat, precut meat distributed in ready-to-serve packages—steaks, chops, and roasts—for sale to hotels, restaurants, and institutions (HRI). The firm started producing boxed beef for the retail grocery market soon after that. IBP actively promoted the innovation to retailers.

Retailers were initially resistant to the program. Packers had directed their original boxed beef programs to the HRI market, and HRI standards are not compatible with retail grocery standards. The biggest difference between the two is that HRI customers have very high profit margins since they are selling the meat cooked, and they have little use for by-products such as trim and so will accept lower yields per side. The retail customers have lower margins and can use some of the by-products. They use trim in sausage and hamburger and sell bones for soup. So retail firms demanded higher yields per side. IBP had initially hoped to expand its HRI line and distribute the product to retailers as well, but the retailers demanded a modification of the innovation before they would accept it. Because there were alternatives available (retailers could continue purchasing sides from other sources), IBP could not force the retailers to adopt the change and so had to compromise.

Since the processing plants used an assembly line, changing the standards involved reorganizing the plant, which was optimized for HRI production. Packers were reluctant to make this change without some assurance that there would be a market for the new product. Wetterau, a large wholesaler, experimented with cutting yields and developed a set of standards, which they then took to the packers. The old specifications were yielding 60% to 70% of the carcass for the retailer. Wetterau developed a new set of standards (largely by including more trim) that would yield 80% to 85% (*PG* August 1971). They convinced the packers to agree to the new specifications. Then Wetterau, IBP, and Grace developed a selling program to convince retailers to adopt the new boxed beef program. The selling program emphasized the following advantages of boxed beef: lower labor costs; lower training costs; better quality control and sanitation; lower transportation, handling, and equipment costs; more merchandising flexibility; and less loss through shrink (spoilage) and purge (dehydration). One store owner emphasized the advantages of boxed beef for the retailer: "We used to buy hinds [quarters] with the result that if you ran [a sale on] both loins and rounds the same week you'd get killed on your gross margin per cent. If you held the rounds until the following week you'd go in and watch the blood drip, drip, drip on the cooler floor—that's weight going out of the rounds and money going out of your pocket. Now [with boxed beef] when we run loins we buy them without the rounds" (*PG* June 1975b). This store owner emphasized the flexibility that boxed beef allowed the retailer. Boxed beef helps to buffer environmental uncertainty for the retailers. The same owner went on to explain the cost benefits of boxed beef: "We've been in box beef almost six years. The first full year of operation I broke all the costs down. Business went up, true; but in the first year I figure I made between $12,000 and $15,000 additional pretax dollars between swinging and box beef" (*PG* June 1975b).

The owner explained that the sources of the cost reduction were less loss from purge and shrinkage, more efficient use of cooler space (sides are very bulky), faster cutting, and lower shipping costs. Table 3.4 breaks down the cost savings of boxed beef versus hanging sides with respect to transportation costs and shrink. Total savings from boxed beef amounted to over 40% of shipping and shrink costs compared to hanging beef. Thus, the innovation did produce the cost savings the retailers needed. These savings came from a combination of reducing the demand uncertainty (due to the ability to buy only the cuts that will sell in that market) and the production uncertainty (the regularization of transportation costs due to the standardized shape and weight of boxed beef).[4] This innovation successfully buffered the retailers' core technologies of shipping and retail cutting from much of the environmental uncertainty (cf. Thompson 1967). The modified boxed beef program was now acceptable to the retailers.

Thus, a coalition consisting of a major wholesaler, the producer of the plastic, and a major meat packer cooperated to modify the innovation so it would be acceptable to the retailers and then set up a program to create a market for the modified innovation. The marketing strategy consisted largely of promoting economic advantages, although there were some arguments along the lines of freeing the retailer from dependence on the meatcutter. One of the benefits of boxed beef was that it enabled a change in the power structure of the retail firm, a change that favored retail management. Since management was responsible for making the decision, this was a strong incentive for adopting the innovation.

In addition to labor cost saving for the retailers, there were also productivity increases in the central plants as a result of the larger volume handled. These plants used a disassembly line to block the sides, resulting in higher output per man hour (see Thompson 1983 for a good description of a meat-packing plant). In addition, the plants used less skilled, lower paid (and often female) workers, further reducing the labor costs of blocking sides (*PG* March 1970, Thompson 1983). A union officer gave his impressions of an IBP plant: "I visited IBP in Iowa back in the early seventies. That plant was the most modern plant in the world. Two-thirds of their work force were women. It was very easy to teach anyone how to cut meat. They were being paid less because they were not journeymen, because they didn't know how to cut it all. They would train people to continuously cut on one item. It may be a piece of chuck or rib or

Table 3.4. Comparison of Handling Costs for Boxed
and Hanging Beef

Freight:		Cost
700-lb. carcass @ .02 / lb		$14.00 / hd
450-lb. Cattle-Pak carcass @ .02 / lb		9.00 / hd
	Savings	$ 5.00 / hd
Shrink:		
Carcass 700-lb. at 0.5% @ 49¢ / lb		$ 1.72 / hd
450-lb. Cattle-Pak		0.00
	Savings	$ 1.72
Total savings		$ 6.72 / hd
	Percent savings	43%

Source: *PG* March 1970

porterhouse, or whatever. It was very easy to teach a person in a short time to make one or two cuts."

The central processing plants took advantage of their high volume to rationalize the production process and to substitute the work of specialized low-status workers in the plants for that of high-status, journeymen meatcutters in the stores. Thus, the change to boxed beef was a classic deskilling innovation (cf. Braverman 1974, Walsh 1989). However, the innovation was not the direct result of management's desire to increase its control over production.

Thus, one of benefits of the innovation was lower costs for the processors. While this did not become part of the argument given to retailers, it does partially explain why the retailers favored the innovation. The benefits the packers would reap from the reduced wage scale allowed them to sell boxed beef at the same price as hanging beef and still make a profit. The wholesalers reaped similar benefits because of the lower handling costs of boxed beef. Sides of beef are very inefficient to store because of their weight and irregular shape.

Worker Response to Boxed Beef

While the new organization of meat production was now acceptable to the packers, wholesalers, retailers, and customers, workers still had to be incorporated into the new system. The introduction of boxed beef struck at one of the core tasks of the meatcutters, blocking sides. As expected, meatcutters in several markets resisted this innovation (*PG* July 1970, *PG* January 1975). A Pittsburgh-based group of independents tested boxed beef in ten stores in 1970. They ran into resistance at the store level. As one wholesaler reported: "We had headquarters personnel visit every store involved trying to show owners, meat managers and meat personnel how the program would help them reapportion their valuable time. Unfortunately, most of the meat department people looked on it as an invasion of their domain and the experiment failed" (*PG* April 1972:175).

Workers in these stores felt that the change was an attack on their core tasks, and so resisted, successfully in this case. One chain took its best meatcutters out of the stores to work in the central plant, so the stores were left without experienced cutters to handle final preparation. The experiment failed and so they went back to shipping sides (*PG* April 1972). This example shows that while the reorganized division of labor reduced the demand for cutters in the stores, it did not eliminate it entirely. Cutters were still an important part of the production process.

In Chicago the meatcutters successfully resisted the introduction of boxed beef throughout the city until 1978. In December 1977, the independent grocers took a strike (the first in 63 years) in order to break away from the pattern agreement covering the city. The strike lasted through the holiday season, the busiest time of the year for retailers, and into the spring and was not settled until the mayor interceded on the independents' behalf. The next contract gave the independents the right to sell boxed beef (*PG* March 1978). Thus, the balance of power was fairly equal between the firms and the union until the firms exercised their political power (in this case in the form of informal pressure from the mayor).

Meatcutters in Chicago were able to resist boxed beef because they were unionized, the union was strong, and they were in a union city. Chicago was the national headquarters for the meatcutters' union. This situation reduced their substitutability. In addition, cutters were highly central to the production process, although becoming less so, as the demand for red meat began to wane during the 1970s and 1980s. Finally, cutters were one part of the organization that absorbed important uncertainties. Even in boxed beef operations, firms needed skilled cutters to maintain production.

Also, because of the market context (all the stores were bound by the same contract), no firm lost market share by not converting to the more productive boxed beef. Since groceries are a local market, as long as all the firms in the city follow the same rules, it does not matter if alternative methods are more productive. Although any firm could reap monopoly profits by adopting the new technology when others do not, the pressure of those profits is outweighed by pressures the union could bring on the firm for attempting the change.

Boxed beef disrupted established in-store routines and eliminated much of the work of the skilled meatcutters in the stores. Workers resisted this attack on their core tasks and were successful in a few markets with very strong unions, such as Chicago, which was the headquarters for the Amalgamated Meat Cutters until 1978. However, the combination of price pressure during the inflationary seventies and decreased consumption of red meat weakened the position of the cutters in the stores. Because red meat was becoming less central to the consumer, the meatcutters had a less central role in the organization. In addition, the innovation itself eliminated part of the basis of the workers' power: it was not easy to find substitutes who knew how to block sides of beef (cf. Burkhardt and Brass 1990).[5] Boxed beef (particularly the boneless variety) is much easier to cut than swinging beef, which reduced the uncertainty in the process and made it easier to find substitutes who could do the work.

I found no evidence of organized resistance by consumers. Consumers probably did not notice the change, because it was a change in process. The product was essentially the same (unlike frozen beef). Similarly, there were few attempts at persuading consumers to accept the innovation (again, unlike frozen beef, which used extensive advertising campaigns). Boxed beef was easier to integrate into the social relations of meat distribution than was frozen meat.

Boxed Beef: Standard Practice

Thus, a combination of technological innovation, price pressure, and a cultural change (less emphasis on red meat) made boxed beef a feasible way of transforming the work in the stores to increase productivity. There was also a series of organizational changes, such as the development of a relationship between the packers and the wholesalers to promote the new technology and the reorganization of the processing plants to satisfy retail standards. Finally, there was an occupational change, as the work was transformed from the domain of skilled journeyman cutters to the domain of semiskilled, female packinghouse workers.

The result was a successful innovation. In 1970 boxed beef accounted for about 20% of total meat sales in the country (PG March 1970). In 1977 boxed beef accounted for over half of all fresh beef sales (excluding ground beef) (Bucklin 1980, PG July 1978). By 1985 boxed beef accounted for over 70% of the market and IBP was the number one supplier (PG June 1985b). Boxed beef has now become standard practice in the industry.

Comparing boxed beef to frozen meat sheds some light on why an innovation succeeds. Both inventions solved the perceived problem of the high cost of in-store processing. However, frozen meat required a major and costly reorganization of the entire meat distribution process, from the packers to the households. Boxed beef only required shifting the task of blocking from the retailers to the packers (a natural extension of the packers' slaughtering and dressing operations) and instituting a relatively simple packaging process, once a stable packaging material was found. In addition, the large size of the major producers of boxed beef did allow them to generate scale economies in the production process, which kept the price of boxed beef competitive with that of hanging beef. The fact that boxed beef did not require costly additions to the tasks or equipment required by the retailers made it much easier to integrate into their production and distribution relations. And because there was no noticeable change in the end product, consumers had no problem integrating the new product into their household economies, so they were largely indifferent to the change.

Boxed beef had to overcome two major problems. The first was finding acceptable standards for the primal cutting. This problem was solved through cooperation between packers and a wholesaler to develop new standards, and then by convincing the retailers to accept these standards. They used an advertising-education program to develop a market for their new product, emphasizing the cost benefits as well as the power benefits to retailers. The large producers of boxed beef (IBP and Missouri Beef) were also in a position to sway retailers because of their size. By 1980 these two packers combined to slaughter more than one-third of the choice grade cattle (the grade generally use for retail meat) and produced approximately 50% of boxed beef (UFCW 1980).[6] While their market share was not enough to prevent retailers from resorting to alternatives, it did give more clout to the packers' suggestions that retailers adopt the boxed-beef program. The second problem boxed beef faced was cutters' resistance. This problem was overcome largely through a political struggle in which the innovation itself helped undermine the cutters' resistance.

One-Stop Shopping in the Meat Department

The increased demand for customer service that surfaced in the late 1970s resulted in two important changes in the meat department reflecting the trend toward more service in the stores: the resurgence of service meat and the addition of delicatessen and seafood departments. Both of these changes reflect the firms' strategy of one-stop shopping. As noted in Chapter 2, firms began expanding the range of products and services offered to fulfill the demand for customer service during this time. This section begins our exploration of the changes toward increased customer service. Chapter 5 gives a more extensive analysis of the effects of these changes on the workers in the new departments.

Service meat counters had become quite scarce during the 1960s, but during the 1970s they began to reappear. By 1981, 36% of stores had service meat counters (*PG* June 1981). However, these new service meat counters are a supplement to, not a replacement for, the self-serve meat case. The new counters are often staffed by customer-service attendants, low-status workers whose technical competence consists primarily of being able to handle customers. These workers have no training in cutting meat and in union shops are not allowed any work involving the tools of the trade.

The second change was the introduction of two new service departments: the deli and seafood departments. Until the early seventies, deli and seafood consisted primarily of prepackaged or frozen product, sold self-serve through the meat department. In the mid-seventies, many chains began installing separate deli and seafood shops. By 1990, 33% of stores had a seafood shop and 71% had a deli (see Table 1.2). The cost of meatcutter labor was too high to use in these labor intensive departments, so the union and the companies compromised. They introduced the classifications of seafood clerk and deli clerk. They were paid less than meatcutters (about the same as meat wrappers), and their duties were limited to their respective departments. Chapter 5 goes into more detail about the development of these service departments.

I found no evidence that the cutters felt threatened by the new departments nor that they tried to keep the new departments out. In fact, some cutters welcomed the new departments because they were an opportunity for cutters who had been displaced by the earlier changes, particularly central processing, to work in shops that were related to meat, even though the work was not of journeyman status. The meatcutters gave up very little when they allowed the introduction of the new departments. The tasks that were involved in operating the new departments were not part of the core of meat cutting. The cutters chose not to expend their energy fighting the introduction of the new occupations.

This new customer-service strategy required workers with competence in customer service, particularly in the service departments. In keeping with this trend toward service, SuperStores had a training program in customer service for workers in the meat departments. The program was designed to increase sales by improving customer-service skills. One store manager observed: "We've started a meat training program. Each meat and seafood employee will go to a two-day seminar. They're not going to tell them how to cut meat or wrap seafood. They're going to tell them how we react or how our department looks to the customer on the other side of the counter; how we bring them back; how we take care of questions. Not standing behind a saw, but what we do out at the case."

While customer-service skills are often considered common sense (see Chapter 5), firms began to realize that the new customer-service tasks were not trivial and were also not part of the meat workers' bundles of tasks. The training programs were an attempt at increasing worker competence in order to increase productivity in terms of sales generated. Thus, when firms diversified, they introduced new tasks into the organization, tasks that were not part of any established bundle. They made up for this lack, in part, through formal training programs.

The one-stop-shopping strategy required an expansion of the roles in the in-store division of labor. These new tasks, in the service meat, deli, and seafood departments, were not part of the existing social relations. Firms created these new departments and then added new roles, which were staffed by low-status workers. Cutters did not resist these innovations because either they were not part of their bundle of tasks or they were very peripheral (stocking frozen fish, for example, used to be part of the cutters' domain). In fact, many of these tasks had already been given over to the less skilled wrappers. In addition to establishing the new roles, firms expanded the role of cutter to include the previously removed customer-service tasks. Cutters did not resist this addition of the low-status task, although they did not embrace it either. Most cutters I talked to felt that this change was largely cosmetic and that they would still spend most of their time in the back room. As for the customers, they seemed to embrace the change in product, because while no existing products were eliminated, additional products were now available.

Summary

Management of a firm has a strong incentive to institute three types of changes—mechanization, Taylorism, and diversification. The meat department experienced all three types of changes. Mechanization increased productivity during a time of rising demand. Cutters did not resist the mechanizations because the changes did not challenge their core tasks. Diversification into full service and delis and seafood shops helped take advantage of established distribution channels and customer base, and the increased demand for service was not resisted by workers. The meat department also experienced both types of Taylorism. The hierarchical division of labor (meat clerks) was embraced by the cutters, because they were freed of a low-status task. The nonhierarchical division of labor (boxed beef) was resisted because it attacked the cutters' core tasks. The cutters were in general unsuccessful in their resistance, except where their monopoly over tasks was particularly well established. This series of changes suggests that Braverman's (1974) arguments about the role of innovation in increasing managerial control and reducing worker skills is, at best, partially correct. While boxed beef was a classic deskilling innovation, other innovations (such as the introduction of power saws) maintained or enhanced workers' skills and control over the production process. Finally, some innovations (such as the employment of meat clerks) increased the division of labor but in such a way that it, at worst, had no effect and, at best, enhanced the status and skills of the cutters.

The meat department, particularly the case of central processing, shows the complexity of technological innovations. Implementing the innovation of boxed beef, for example, required coordination by plastics manufacturers, meat packers, wholesalers, retailers, customers, and (reluctantly) the cutters. Implementing frozen meat would have required a major reorganization of packers', wholesalers', retailers', cutters', and customers' routines. The complexity of this innovation, which was based on a relatively straightforward invention, was one reason for its failure. This suggests that innovations that are less disruptive are more likely to be adopted. Following March and Simon's (1958) arguments about organizations as satisficers, this also suggests that, when faced with two innovations that equally satisfy minimal requirements for reducing a performance gap, firms will adopt the less disruptive of the two, even if the other innovation might produce better results. The case of the new service departments shows that organizational innovations also require reorganizing the social relations to implement the new strategy. In this case, firms added new categories of workers (deli and seafood clerks) as well as supplementing the cutter's bundle of tasks to include customer-service skills—skills that had been eliminated by the shift to self-service 30 years before.

4

COMPUTERIZATION IN THE SUPERMARKETS

DURING THE 1970S and 1980s supermarkets joined the high-tech revolution. They began to incorporate computer technology into their store operations. While firms in the industry had long used mainframe computers for such administrative tasks as payroll, they now were beginning to incorporate computers into the daily tasks of the shop-floor employees.

The most significant impact of computers on in-store operations was initiated by the implementation of bar-code readers and price lookup systems—the scanners. These devices revolutionized work on the front end (the checkout stand) of the supermarket and also came to be one of the most visible representations of computers for the public. Firms also started using computers to alleviate some of the more cumbersome paperwork in the stores, such as keeping track of employee time cards and ordering inventory (*PG* January 1986a). Other uses of computers, such as for inventory control, are still in the testing stage, so their impact on the industry is not yet clear. This chapter will concentrate on the development and implementation of scanners, the use of computerized ordering systems, and their effects on workers in the stores.

Some have argued that new, computer-based technologies have expanded the opportunities for managers to transform the labor process. Zuboff's (1988) analysis of the effects of computer technology on several factory and office settings leads her to conclusions that echo Braverman's (1974). She argues that workers are unable to maintain the same mastery over automated technology as they had over previous technology because automation devalues direct experience and emphasizes the novel (to shop-floor workers) domain of abstract reasoning. This problem is exacerbated by management's desire to maintain control. So, for example, the computer interfaces are deliberately made obscure in order to make it difficult for workers to master the technology. Shaiken (1984) made a similar observation about the languages used to program numerically controlled machine tools.[1] Also, managers justify their investment in the new technology by laying off workers and pointing to the labor savings generated by the innovations (Zuboff 1988:249). Zuboff shows that such changes also solidify management's authority, which is grounded in mastery of the abstract. In addition, information-based technology creates a new level of technical control, which Zuboff refers to as the panopticon. The panopticon combines the surveillance aspects of direct control with the obfuscating aspects of technical control. The reversal in control that Marx claims occurred during the shift from tools, which workers controlled, to machines, which controlled workers, has so evolved that automated machines not only direct the production process but also perform the foreman's function of reporting on the worker's degree of adherence to his or her limited role. According to Shaiken (1984), managers have also tried to use computer technology to automate batch process manufacturing to the point where it approaches the continuous process manufacturing systems described by Zuboff. Flexible manufacturing systems (FMS), robots, and management information systems (MIS) are all designed to minimize worker input and maximize management control over direct production.

My analysis of computerization in the supermarkets will show only limited support for such arguments. Management in the supermarkets used computers mainly to automate the more routine work in the stores. While this automation did reduce the demand for workers, the same technology also allowed an upgrading of certain workers, as some of the tasks that were previously part of the manager's bundle were given to shop-level employees as a result of the introduction of computers.

The Development and Implementation of Scanners

The introduction of scanners into grocery stores was the result of a series of experiments and compromises between equipment manufacturers, product manufacturers, food retailers, consumers, and the labor union. While there were technical problems that had to be solved for scanning to be successful, there were equally important social problems that had to be negotiated. The industry and its suppliers needed to develop a set of standards that would allow all the suppliers to produce symbols that all the scanners could read. In addition, retailers had to overcome both the union's and the consumers' objections to the new system.

Market Context

Retailers faced declining profits and rising wages in the late 1960s and early 1970s. These conditions should have led to attempts to cut labor costs. Mechanization and centralization in the meat department are examples of cost-cutting innovations that resulted from a profit squeeze. Another means of reducing labor costs is automation (Wallace and Kalleberg 1982). Before the advent of computers, some of the most labor-intensive aspects of a supermarket involved keeping track of the prices of goods. The combination of self-service, the large number of different items in a supermarket (more than 16,000 in an average store in 1990 [*PG* April 1991]), and the variation in the mix of goods that each customer buys makes it crucial for the firms to have some way to identify the price of each item and then to sum those prices to determine the price of a basket of goods (cf. Stinchcombe 1990). Until the mid-1970s, this procedure was done by hand. Stockers took cases of goods off the truck, priced each item in the case, and put the priced goods on the shelves. A customer picked up goods, was able to compare the prices of items, and decided whether or not to buy the item. A checker then looked at the price markers on the customer's items and entered the prices into the cash register. The cash register totaled the prices and gave the cashier the total for that basket. The customer then paid the cashier the total and took the items home.

This transaction was quite labor intensive. As Glazer (1984) notes, now much of the labor is done by the customer, a major innovation in the retail food industry that occurred primarily during the profit squeeze of the 1930s (Zimmerman 1955). However, faced with declining profits and increased labor costs, firms had an incentive to eliminate further paid in-store labor. Retailers looked for ways to automate this process if possible. Scanners had the potential to accomplish this automation.

Scanners are systems for automating the process of attaching a price to a given item. By marking the item in some computer-readable form, then attaching a reader to a computer with a lookup program and hooking this into the cash register, the checker can have the scanner read the item and enter the price into the register automatically.[2] By having the lookup code attached at the manufacturing plant (or some other central location), retailers can save the cost of having the stockers mark each item. In addition, scanners could potentially buffer retailers from one type of environmental uncertainty, price inflation. Under the previous systems, stockers had to remove the old price and add the new price to each item every time the price changed. As inflation increased during the 1970s, this cost became increasingly significant.[3]

While such a system would reduce in-store labor, this description of the scanners suggests some of the difficulties in developing such a system. One major problem is integrating the routines of the scanner suppliers, the food suppliers (canners, etc.), and the retailers. This problem is aggravated by the fact that the retail market and the food supplier markets are very diffuse. The market for cash registers, however, is much more concentrated (a four-firm concentration ratio of 78% in 1972 [US Census 1977]).

Political Contingencies

While retailers had an incentive to transform in-store tasks to automate the price system, they were likely to face resistance from two contingencies, clerks and consumers. The clerks would oppose such a system because it eliminated much of their labor. They may have had some power to block such an innovation because they were fairly heavily unionized (about 40% during the 1970s). In addition, clerks make up a large part of the total in-store labor force. For example, in two stores for which I have complete data, 40% of the workers were either grocery clerks or cashiers (Table 1.3).[4] Also, the union is large in absolute terms. In 1976 the Retail Clerks International had 700,000 members, making it one of the largest unions in the country. After the 1979 merger with the Amalgamated Meat Cutters, the renamed United Food and Commercial Workers (UFCW) became the largest union in the AFL-CIO. Current membership is 1.3 million. Thus, clerks, while not as skilled as the meatcutters, have some power based on their large numbers. It is difficult to get a large number of replacements at short notice, even if they do not need to be highly skilled (low substitutability).

Customer resistance to price removal was due in part to a general resistance to change and in part to the volatility of prices during the mid-1970s, which made it more difficult for customers to keep track of what goods should cost. In addition, customers distrusted retailers because they believed that high prices were the result of price gouging by the retailers. There was evidence that the increase in prices was due partly to the increase in local concentration in retail food (Lamm 1981, Marion 1979). Finally, goods without prices marked on them make the task of shopping (which is in part the task of maximizing the amount and quality of goods purchased within a given budget) more difficult, since it is harder for consumers to keep track of the value of the goods they choose or to compare the prices of various goods.[5] Also, at this time, consumers had discovered the power of collective action, through both voice and exit (Hirschman 1970), which made them a more substantial force.

Thus, we would expect firms to try to develop systems to automate the pricing function. However, such a system is likely to require collective action between retailers and suppliers to develop standards. We would therefore expect some new relationships to develop between retailers and suppliers to create and maintain such standards. We would expect that customers would have mixed reactions to the innovation. If the change reduced prices, customers should favor it. On the other hand, if the change increased costs to customers (in lost price awareness, for example), customers should resist. Clerks should resist the change, as it is a direct attack on their interests. In addition, they are organized and so have the ability to act and some hope of success.

Automation: Scanners

Scanning was technologically ready for implementation in 1972 (Bucklin 1980). However, the invention still required a rearrangement of the social order to make it feasible. In 1970 product manufacturers and retailers set up the Ad Hoc Committee on Universal Product Codes, with representatives from the major retailer and product manufacturer associations, to develop a set of standards. There was a conflict between the two groups over the form of the codes. Retailers wanted shorter codes because they would make bookkeeping easier; manufacturers wanted longer codes because they would accommodate more products. The form of the symbol was another subject of discussion. Retailers favored symbols that were cheaper to read but more expensive to produce, such as magnetic symbols; manufacturers favored symbols that were cheaper to produce, such as printed symbols that required an optical scanner.

In 1972, the committee decided to adopt a 10-digit code, the Universal Product Code (UPC), as the standard (*PG* January 1972). An optically scannable, printed version of the code eventually won out as the most feasible, primarily because of the high cost per item of magnetic or embossed symbols. There were also two options for the scanners, bottom and hand held. Hand held is easier to develop, because the cashier can put the wand right up to the label, while a bottom scanner has to be able to read at an angle. But bottom scanners allow the checker to have both hands free, increasing her productivity since she can scan with both hands.[6] Since one of the major reasons for the scanners was to speed checkout, the bottom scanner was the preferred system. Today, bottom scanners are by far the more popular.

The first operational scanning of the UPC began on June 26, 1974, at the Troy, Ohio, unit of Marsh Supermarkets, a 129-store chain. The store used registers and a computer from NCR with the scanners.

The choice of Troy, Ohio, was no accident. Troy is the headquarters of Hobart, the maker of scales, UPC label printers, and applicators for in-store marking; and Troy is only a half hour from Dayton, the headquarters of NCR. This well-publicized experiment shows the importance of supplier cooperation in implementing innovations. By setting up scanning in a store nearby, the suppliers could make sure the experiment was successful.

At that time, about 70% of the items were marked with the code. Twenty-seven percent were source marked, and 43% were marked by the store. At the same time as the introduction of the scanners, electronic cash registers were introduced. Electronic registers alone provided an 8% faster throughput without scanning. With scanning, the increase was 12% to 14%, with 45% of units scanned. As the percentage of items scanned increased, productivity also increased. With 90% scanning, the expected increase in productivity, including the increase from the electronic register, was 30% (*PG* March 1975). Also, as the number of items premarked by the manufacturers increased, the costs of the operation would decline. In 1975, it was estimated that an averaged-sized store with $140,000 per week in sales would save $119,000 per year with scanners (Levin et al. 1985). About half of these savings came from reduced labor at checkout. Other savings came from not pricing and fewer checkout errors. In 1978, the cost to implement the system was about $11,000 per checkout lane, with the cost to an average store being about $110,000–$130,000 (Coyle 1978). Since the cost is recovered in about one year, scanning should have been a high-priority innovation. Scanners did provide the desired increase in productivity for the stores.

Thus, the development of the innovation required a compromise and cooperation between retailers, food manufacturers, and computer manufacturers. However, scanners also upset the set of relationships between firms, workers, and consumers (cf. Child 1985). Customers and the union both resisted the introduction of scanners, for different, but complementary, reasons. One of the major sources of the productivity increase from scanners was that cashiers could check out groceries faster, about 30% to 50% faster. However, the other major advantage of scanners was that since the computer read the price from the UPC symbol, there was no need to mark prices on individual items, resulting in enormous labor savings. Stockers would not have to mark individual items before putting them on the shelves. Instead, stores would provide shelf tags with the item name and price. In addition, stockers would not have to remove prices and replace them with the new price every time prices changed, a frequent occurrence during this period. It was price removal that became the locus of the conflict over scanners. Consumers feared that companies would use the scanners to manipulate prices. The union feared that scanners would reduce the demand for clerks.

Customer Response to Scanners

When firms introduced scanners, there was quite a bit of customer resistance because customers did not trust computerized price retrieval. The Troy store noted above surveyed its customers for their reaction to price removal. The survey asked if they would accept price removal in exchange for lower prices. They found that given the choice between price removal and savings, 59% of customers surveyed said price removal was, "OK if it resulted in some savings to the customer"; 16% said, "OK only if it resulted in large savings"; and 25% said, "Prices should be left on regardless of savings" (PG December 1975). The 25% who rejected price removal outright represent a large minority in a business as competitive as supermarkets, especially when competitors were pricing. Since customer loyalty to firms is generally quite low in retail food, firms could not afford to offend 25% of their clientele (Kirstein 1950).[7]

This resistance to scanners was not just the result of the novelty of the technology. The above survey was conducted in 1975. In 1985, SuperStores introduced scanners to one of its stores and got the same type of resistance from the customers. The following quote from a department head in a store that had just introduced scanners shows the resistance of customers to the system, particularly the no-pricing aspects:

Head Produce: We went to scanners four months ago. One of the biggest things that people had complaints about was that we had stopped pricing some items. Not all, but some items that were hard to price, baby food and things like that. They saw the trend. There was a program, and if there hadn't been such dissent from the customers, there was a program to gradually work in till where nothing's priced in the store. . . . At our store it just isn't working out. To me, that's one of the things that hurts [non-pricing competitor] a lot. People won't shop a store where the things aren't priced.

Q: Why do you think they're like that?

Head Produce: People just don't trust computers and the scanners. . . . They might not catch the error at that time, but when they come home, they check the bill, cause everything's printed out, the item name, the price. At least if the product's priced they can check if they weren't cheated. You can't do that, as fast as you're scanning that stuff, there's no way. . . . I guess it's just a basic mistrust, whether it's being mispriced or being rung incorrectly at the register.

This quote emphasizes the importance of demand factors in determining technological changes. SuperStores followed a mixed strategy. When they opened a store in a new city, they would open without pricing and these stores were generally successful. However, when they tried to remove prices in one of their established markets, there was great resistance by the customers, so they returned to pricing items. Like the department head, a division manager in the same market also emphasized customer resistance to price removal:

Division Manager: [Here] we still price, because we're an established, mature area. If you want to ask me would I like to do price removal, the answer is yes. We have experimented with it and our customers complain.

Q: The customer backlash overcomes the benefits?

Division Manager: Absolutely. If the customers tell us they don't want it, we're not going to do it.

While price removal was technologically feasible, it was not acceptable to customers. In this case, customers showed their dissatisfaction in part through voice, by complaining to stores or by giving negative opinions on surveys. This firm's mixed strategy also showed the difference between exit and entry. While customers in new markets were willing to establish relations with a nonpricing store, customers in established markets threatened exit if the store removed prices, suggesting that there is a conservatism in relationships. In addition to the transaction cost aspects of not wanting to change, there is also a feeling of violation of the normative order when actors attempt to reorganize the existing social relations. Thus, the same set of relationships are not necessarily equally viable in different settings.

Worker Response to Scanners

Consumer groups feared price manipulation with the advent of scanning. Unions feared the job loss, both at the checkout counter (the higher productivity would reduce the demand for cashiers) and in the stock room (there would be no labor spent pricing and changing prices—a large percentage of the stocker's day). By fighting price removal instead of scanning per se, unions could form a coalition with a powerful ally, activist consumer groups, as well as invoke the consumer in the abstract in ideological debates in such forums as state legislatures. The Clerks Union has a history of taking grievances to the consumer as a means of extending the workers' power (Harrington 1962, Kirstein 1950). The union would probably be less successful opposing scanning on the grounds that increased productivity at the front end would hurt them, because the union's loss would be a benefit to consumers as well as to companies. In adopting the no-price strategy as a compromise position, the union appeared to be reasonable in the face of new technology and also gained public support for its position, since it was fighting as, or in the name of, consumers. If the union had fought scanning per se, on the other hand, it would have openly opposed advancements in productivity (and increased customer service) through new technology. The president of the Clerks Union gave the union position on pricing in an interview in *Progressive Grocer:*

> Retail Clerks President: Our 700,000 members are consumers, too, and I think they're right in joining other consumers in insisting on being able to price compare with prices stamped on every piece of merchandise. Mistakes can be made with computer pricing you know. How does the consumer know she's not paying more than she should? How can she remember what price was on the shelf?

I've seen store managers under great pressure from supervisors to show a good return. Put people under pressure like that and they may be tempted to turn UPC computer pricing to their advantage. It could happen. (*PG* April 1976)

Thus, as we would expect, workers resisted this innovation, since it was attacking their core tasks, checking and pricing. By selectively attacking the innovation in the areas where the union was strongest (price removal), the members were able to form a coalition with consumers and to petition the state to set favorable rules that would be followed in the implementation of the innovation. The workers' power in this case comes from the fact that they were hard to replace, because they are unionized and therefore can act in concert, because they held a central position in the organization (stocking and checking were the main tasks of retailers), and because they were allied with a powerful actor. This power allowed the union to modify the form of innovation such that the workers did not incur as much of the costs of the innovation.

Scanners: Partially Standard Practice

Scanners were first introduced in 1974. By 1975, there were only 40 stores in the country with scanning. But the price-removal plans, which were a major selling point of the technology to retailers, came during a time when inflation was high and consumer groups were active. Resistance took the form of direct action by consumers (such as not buying from nonpricing stores and complaining to store managers) and by unions (such as negotiating job-security clauses into their contracts). Consumer groups aided by the union also fought for pricing legislation at the local, state, and national levels. By December 1975, Connecticut, California, and Rhode Island had already passed mandatory price-marking legislation, and Massachusetts had an existing law that in effect required pricing. Some cities, Chicago, for example, had also passed such laws (*PG* December 1975). Michigan and New York followed soon after (Coyle 1978).

In September 1975, retailers and manufacturers in California who were experimenting with scanning were granted a two-year moratorium from the state legislature on price-marking legislation so they could test the scanners and show they had no ill effects on the consumers (*PG* September 1975). However, shortly after that moratorium was passed, consumer resistance to the no-pricing policies led to price-marking legislation in California, overriding the moratorium (*PG* December 1975).

Industry leaders hoped a voluntary move to keep prices on would head off mandatory price legislation. Giant Foods, a Mid-Atlantic chain, put prices back on at their scanning test store in Severna Park, Maryland. They estimated their price-off program had been saving them 23%–30% of labor costs on stocking (*PG* May 1975). However, the potential loss from consumer action was considered even greater.

Thus, while the technical problems of scanning had largely been overcome, there were significant problems with the social relations of the new technology. While price removal is not a necessary part of a scanning system, firms had a strong incentive to encourage price removal to increase productivity. However, consumer resistance, particularly when it became embodied in legislation, prevented firms from introducing all the aspects of the scanning system. Consumers were reacting to the product change (removing prices) rather than the process change (scanning at the checkout). Consumer power in this case came from unequal substitutability. Large numbers of customers who were offended by nonpricing policies could easily find other firms who were pricing. However, firms who removed prices could not easily pick up large numbers of new customers. Also, consumers and the union took advantage of the open-systems nature of the organizations to move their protests to an arena where they were likely to have more success, state legislatures. Consumers and unions together make up relatively large constituencies when compared to retailers, and legislators were already sympathetic to pleas to limit retailer actions that might increase price (Marion 1979). For example, retail food was one of the last industries to be released from wage-and-price controls in the early 1970s.

The union and consumers have been moderately effective in fighting price removal. In exchange for allowing the introduction of scanners, in 1975 Giant Foods guaranteed the union that no clerk would lose his job or be downgraded (*PG* December 1975, *PG* January 1975).

In 1980, Giant became the first chain to implement scanning for 100% of its stores (*PG* April 1980). About 60% of SuperStores have adopted nonpricing. Thus, consumer resistance and union activity were sufficiently strong in at least some markets to modify the firms' strategies for introducing the new technology. By 1989, 15 years after scanners were first introduced, eight states still had individual-item price-marking legislation, and the issue is still being debated in state legislatures (*Buffalo News* July 24, 1989). I do not have sufficient data to specify the conditions under which consumers or unions in one market succeeded while those in other markets failed, or did not even resist the change. It would be interesting to collect data by market on the number of stores not pricing to see if these differences could be explained by differences in market concentration, consumer activity, and union strength.

In general, SuperStores' strategy of slowly phasing out prices in established markets and not putting prices in new markets seems quite successful. Consumer loyalty to grocery firms seems quite sensitive to services offered as well as to price. Consumers will resist shopping at a store that doesn't price when an alternative store is available that does price and has similar prices. However, increased store size, higher wages, and cheaper scanners will all increase the cost (and price) difference between scanning and nonscanning stores. In addition, as more stores adopt the innovation, the probability of having a nonscanning competitor decreases. And as consumers become more accustomed to scanners, they will be less resistant to the change. All of these factors reduce the costs to the retailer, in terms of customer resistance, of not pricing. Also, as prices stabilized during the 1980s, consumer fears of price manipulation decreased, since it was easier to keep track of prices. As the union loses its consumer allies, it is more difficult for the union to resist price removal. In addition, union strength is declining (*PG* April 1987). Thus, the combination of a change in the cost effectiveness of scanning and a change in the historical context of scanning—from a period of inflation, lots of consumer activity, and a strong union to stable prices, declining consumer activity, and a weaker union—has led to an increase in price removal. However, price removal lagged well behind scanning because firms had to overcome the social problems as well as the technical ones. Currently, about 62% of store sales are scanned (*PG* October 1989). Scanning has become standard practice. However, the question of item pricing has still not been settled. In 1988, 50% of stores still price marked individual items (*PG* April 1989).

Computerization, Increased Store Size, and the Diffusion of Management Tasks

The spread of the UPC symbol facilitated the spread of computerization to other parts of the store. One important change that followed from the computerized price lookup system was computerized ordering based on the UPC. This innovation required the invention of a machine that could computerize the ordering tasks. Suppliers developed several versions of computerized ordering systems, generally consisting of a hand-held computer for entering the order and a mainframe connection to process the order. This section will describe the task of ordering before computerization and then describe how computerization changed it. In addition, I will show how this system interacted with the increase in store size to decentralize operations in the stores.

Before computerization, the person ordering would inspect the aisles with a book in hand that listed the products in order by product code. For each product, he would check the amount on the shelf and how much was in the back room, then find the product in the order book, and note how many he wanted for the next delivery.[3] This task involved lots of searching through the book, since the order in the book did not correspond to the grouping on the shelves. When he finished marking the order, the person ordering would either mail or call in the order to the office. The computerized ordering machines greatly reduced ordering time and simplified the ordering process. The ordering machine is generally a small box with a numeric keypad and an optional scanning wand. The person ordering either types in or scans the UPC and types in the quantity needed of that product. After finishing the order, he plugs the machine into a

Table 4.1. Responses by Department Heads to the Question:
"What Is the Most Difficult Part of Your Job?" (Open Ended)

Response	Percent responding
Employee relations / scheduling	41%
Ordering	29
"Getting it all done"	12
Other	18
Total	100% (N=17)

modem and dials the office computer. The computer then transfers the order electronically and forwards it to the warehouse. One study found that computerized ordering not only cut ordering time in half but also increased accuracy (*PG* March 1985).

One result of the increase in store size and firm size and the introduction of computer technology has been the increasing division of labor of management responsibilities. The job of ordering is one of the most difficult tasks in the store (cf. Stinchcombe 1990). For example, when I asked department heads, "What is the most difficult part of your job?" ordering was the second most common response, with 29% saying it was the most difficult (see Table 4.1). Part of this difficulty is due to the arcane paperwork requirements. Ordering requires the department head to know the location of every item in the order book. There were more than 16,000 different items in a typical grocery store in 1990 (*PG* April 1991). The largest stores can stock more than 60,000 items (*PG* December 1984). Not only is there a lack of correlation between the placement of items in the store and the order in the book, there are also several books from which to order. One book contains items from one vendor or warehouse, while one aisle may contain items from several vendors or warehouses. Part of the difficulty of ordering is also due to the problem of maximizing sales while minimizing inventory, the problem of matching local demand. In addition, department heads want to be able to take advantage of price specials by suppliers to increase profits by buying cheap and selling dear. Chapter 5 expands on the problems of matching local demand and manipulating inventories.

The use of computerized ordering facilitated store expansion by reducing the time taken to process the ordering of a given product.

Ordering and keeping track of orders are very time-consuming processes. Expanding product lines required an ever-increasing amount of time to process the information for the lines, so firms had to devote more resources to ordering. And most of this additional time is for tasks previously under the domain of the store manager. Stocking time is determined largely by the total number of items, rather than the number of different items. Ordering time, on the other hand, is determined mainly by the number of different items, not the total number of items. While it takes about the same amount of time to stock 120 cans of tomato soup or 24 cans each of 5 varieties of soup, it takes roughly 5 times as long to order the mixed lot as it does to order the 120 cans of one variety.[9] In addition, ordering requires two kinds of competence: knowing how much to order based on past experience and expected trends and knowing how to process the paperwork. As the number of products in the mix increases, it becomes more difficult to have enough knowledge of the first type to order successfully. But workers who ordered often cited learning the paperwork as the part of their job that took the longest to learn. The computerized ordering machine reduces the amount of paperwork, freeing those with less knowledge of paperwork but with greater knowledge of product movement—those closer to the shelves—to do the ordering, thus alleviating the problem of accurately predicting local demand.

In fact more and more of the responsibility for ordering has been delegated to department heads and even to the more senior clerks. For example, while ordering for the grocery department used to be the domain of the head grocery clerk, now he would give each of the senior clerks responsibility for ordering, as well as stocking and maintaining, one or two aisles in the store. By spreading out the ordering, the organization can handle a greater mix of products because no one person needs to know about a large number of products. By reorganizing the distribution of tasks in the store, the organization could take advantage of worker knowledge and expand the size of the stores. Workers did not resist this change because this was an increase in the number of tasks in their domain, and the added task (ordering) was a high-status activity. In fact, workers viewed this change positively. Workers took pride in their new responsibility for all aspects of "their aisle."

The introduction of the computerized ordering machine facilitated the diffusion of the management task of ordering by reducing the paperwork requirements for ordering, making it easier to train someone in the mechanics of ordering, and allowing the store to take advantage of the specific knowledge of the stockers who know which products sell and which do not by how often they refill the shelves and what is piled up in the back room.

Thus, rather than concentrating information that workers collect in the hands of management, supermarkets have diffused knowledge that was once the exclusive domain of management among the workers. It is inefficient for one person to order all of the merchandise in a large store. Managers cannot keep track of all the product movement, inventory, and deals for the tens of thousands of products in a large store, particularly since the one-stop-shopping strategy has increased the range of products considerably. SuperStores has transferred these competences from the domain of management to the domain of workers.

The example of the computerized ordering machine shows how a new invention (the computerized ordering machine) can, when combined with market changes and firm changes (one-stop-shopping strategy), lead to a reorganization of the in-store relationships, the creation of a decentralized structure. Unlike the cases cited in the deskilling literature, however, this reorganization led to an increase in worker competence, as firms decentralized the high-status task of ordering to the stockers. The next chapter discusses in more detail the effects on the workers of this decentralization.

This example also shows how innovations build on each other. The implementation of scanners and the UPC created a context that greatly facilitated the automation of the mechanics of ordering. The same innovation that speeded up the checkers also facilitated the upgrading of the stockers.

Summary

Computerization has been shown to have very drastic effects on work organization (Noble 1984, Shaiken 1984, Zuboff 1988). Computerization is a special type of mechanization, because while it still tends to automate fairly routine tasks (matching the price to an item, matching an item to its order number), computerization also has the potential to eliminate more fundamental tasks (Nobel 1984, Zuboff 1988). Like previous industries studied, the supermarket industry has been affected by the spread of the computer. Unlike those previously cited, the computer has not had particularly devastating effects on the workers' tasks, although scanners did drastically reduce the demand for these workers. The two major computer-based innovations have been the scanner and the computerized ordering machine. The case of the scanners, like that of boxed beef, shows the complexity of implementing an innovation. The change required the cooperation of retailers, food manufacturers, and computer companies. This change was also resisted by workers (because it attacked their core tasks) and consumers (because price removal was a product change). Workers were partially successful in their alliance with consumers and have managed to get price-marking legislation and voluntary pricing policies in several markets.

The computerized ordering machine, on the other hand, was an innovation that expanded worker skills and that was not resisted and indeed was even welcomed by workers. It automated a routine task (paperwork) and, in the context of increasing store size, facilitated the decentralization of ordering responsibilities.

Both of these cases illustrate the importance of context in determining the nature of an innovation and its effects on work organization. The next section explores the effects of context on organizational innovations that move tasks from management to the workers.

5

DIVERSIFICATION AND ITS EFFECT ON
THE SHOP FLOOR

THIS CHAPTER EXPLORES the development of an organizational innovation. There has been a variety of changes in the market context of stores during the last few decades. Firms have moved into more regions, stores have become larger, customers have begun to demand more service, and profits have declined. The proposed solution to the problem of competition in this new environment was the adoption of the one-stop-shopping diversification strategy. Like the centralization of meat cutting and the adoption of scanning technology, this diversification strategy created problems of implementation. In particular, firms were entering markets that required skills not previously required by store-level employees. Also, there was a problem of information flows in the new departments—the problem of local demand. SuperStores responded to this challenge by decentralizing operations. This decentralization created problems of governance and worker skill. The solution to both problems was making each department a profit center and giving the department head responsibility for training and for performance. The following sections describe the development of the decentralized structure at SuperStores, and how this structure overcomes the problems of opportunism and training. The chapter concludes with an analysis of worker skill in the new departments, in particular, the relationship between competence, status, and gender.

Decentralization of SuperStores

The following section describes the market context and the political contingencies that led to the decentralization of SuperStores. This decentralization went through several stages; first the divisions, then the stores, and eventually the store clerks were allowed more autonomy and responsibility.

The Market Context

As supermarkets grew, as firms spread over several regions, and as firms diversified into new lines, these factors combined to upset the web of relations in the stores. Much of the increase in task complexity that the diversification strategy created fell within the store manager's domain. However, this put a substantial burden on the store managers. This burden was compounded by the fact that fewer store managers had been store clerks and so had limited experience with the details of store operations. Finally, since many of the new lines were novel for grocery stores (bakeries, seafood shops, floral shops, restaurants), store managers were unlikely to have had significant experience with these departments. To overcome these limits on the store manager's ability to process the necessary information (mainly predicting customer preferences and understanding operations for the production departments), SuperStores began extending more control to the shop-floor level—department heads and store clerks. In organizational theory there is a substantial literature that emphasizes the need to adopt a more decentralized structure in the face of a more complex environment (Burns and Stalker 1961, Galbraith 1973, Lawrence and Lorsch 1967). Chapter 4 showed that one result of this expansion and diversification strategy has been the decentralization of ordering tasks to the department heads and store clerks. This chapter will elaborate on several other aspects of the decentralized structure.

Political Contingencies

For organizational restructuring, the political actors will generally be departments of the firm. Pfeffer (1981) describes the power relations among departments for several organizational innovations. Chandler (1962) describes the power struggles between the general office and the divisions that accompanied attempts to reorganize at General Motors, for example. Structural reorganizations generally favor one department or division over others (Burkhardt and Brass 1990) and these divisions will attempt to use their centrality, their control over uncertainty, or their irreplaceability as leverage for advancing their interests (Hickson et al. 1971).

I focused my research on data collection at the store level and so have little data on the relations among, for example, the operations managers and perishables managers at the division or corporate levels of the management hierarchy (cf. McGlaughlin, German, and Uetz 1986). Lacking sufficient data on the political contingencies, this chapter will focus on the market context and the changes in the web of relations in the stores. A given market context can lead to a variety of possible compatible innovations. The particular form of innovation depends on the political contingencies and on the existing web of relations. In the present case, the market context made a centralized organization less viable. SuperStores responded to this change in context by decentralizing. However, the exact form of the decentralization—in particular, the relations at the division and corporate level—was probably heavily influenced by existing relations and political contingencies.

The Development of Decentralization

Given the change in market context, we would expect SuperStores to adopt a more decentralized structure. We would also expect that, given the cross-store market variance, that this decentralization would be to the store level. This section traces the development of decentralization in SuperStores over the last 50 years.

As SuperStores expanded over the years, it modified its structure several times to accommodate its new environment. SuperStores, like many firms during that time adopted a multidivisional form in the 1930s (cf. Chandler 1962, Fligstein 1985). Because the chain was growing, it reorganized again in 1955, giving the divisions more control over operations. Each of three division heads was given the title of division vice president and was responsible for a unit with annual sales of $20 million to $150 million (1955 dollars). The corporation added five corporate vice presidents, to bring its total to eight corporate vice presidents, in addition to the president. This corporate committee developed company policy and objectives, with the divisions implementing those policies. This structure is very similar to the multidivisional form described by Chandler (1962). SuperStores also implemented an incentive bonus plan for store managers. The strategy of SuperStores was described in its 1959 annual report:

> Decentralization is being extended to the stores. The average store, with its annual volume of $1,357,885, represents a sizeable business in itself. Capable management at the store level is required to take advantage of local merchandising opportunities. Through our continuing recruiting and training programs the caliber of management has been greatly improved.
> Store managers are encouraged to exercise initiative in adapting the operation of their stores to the customers they serve and to develop merchandising programs in terms of their neighborhoods. They are assisted by specialists from the division office, especially in the field of perishables. They are authorized to meet local competitive situations. Incentive bonus plans and participation in the company profit sharing program develops a financial interest in the results they accomplish.

The increase in the size and geographic dispersion of the Super-Stores chain led to a need to give more autonomy to the division and the store managers. Lawrence (1958) describes a similar decentralization to the store manager in another supermarket chain, at about the same time. The annual report shows that the corporate management of SuperStores recognized that different stores faced different environmental conditions, for example, the demand particulars of each store's neighborhood.

In 1969, the firm reorganized again, this time as a result of its diversification into new lines (drugstores, combination food and soft goods stores, and food processing) and their strategy of building ever larger stores. It created five separate management groups: food stores, food processing, drugstores, combination stores, and trading stamps.

In addition, like many corporations during this period, more general office executives were from nonoperations backgrounds (Chandler 1962, Katz 1987, Wright 1979). Fligstein (1985) notes that getting a president from finance or sales is one factor that leads to the adoption of the multidivisional form. In 1962, a new president began serving SuperStores. He had joined the company in 1944 as a vice president. However, his previous experience was in politics, including time as a state representative and a congressman. He was succeeded in 1970 by a vice president who had joined the company as the result of a merger with a drugstore chain and who was in charge of the drug division. In the late 1970s, SuperStores' president was a man who had come up from the stores. However, the current president worked his way through the corporate affairs division, a staff division. Thus, three out of the last four presidents did not have grocery store backgrounds.

Beginning in 1971, SuperStores conducted a series of studies over 10 years to analyze the role of the store manager in the new, larger stores. The studies showed that the increase in store size and the decentralized structure put an enormous burden on the store managers. To make store managers more effective, SuperStores reorganized in-store management to create the functional division of management shown in Figure 1.2. This change was accompanied by increased training of managers, especially in communications skills and strategic planning. Part of the new structure included an increase in the autonomy of the department heads and store employees.[1] In particular, the firm gave store-level employees more operations autonomy.

These store-level departments had a high degree of autonomy because the increased store size requires store managers to spend less time on direct control. A store with 12 departments, 100–200 employees, and 2–3 shifts per day is too much for one person to supervise directly. Even with functional assistant managers (see Figure 1.2), much of the work is unsupervised. In addition, very few store managers have a background in specialty shops. This is in part a cohort effect, since the shops are relatively new. In part, this is a bias toward grocery and produce. Using data from another chain, Bielby (1991) found that most store managers had backgrounds in grocery or produce departments. My observations at SuperStores also suggest this. This situation is likely due to two factors. First, these two departments are two of the larger ones in the store. Second, they are the male-dominated departments.

Not only are employees from specialty shops underrepresented among store-trained managers, there are increasingly fewer store-trained managers. This increase in college-trained managers comes from the increased emphasis by SuperStores on the managerial aspects of the job, rather than the foreman aspects (see also *PG* May 1987). The director of operations for one of SuperStores' divisions estimated that 70% of new managers came out of college, versus 30% 10 years ago. He went on to elaborate on this change in management recruitment:

> Division Manager: More and more of our managers we're looking at for their people skills, communications skill. We actually have taken an abnormal amount of communications majors and been very successful with their results. We look at people who are people oriented to run our stores. With that base we feel we can work on the technical skills a lot easier. We look for people now who are risk takers. Before, we looked for people who would follow the numbers. Before, they were given the direction from this office and they were asked to follow. They were strictly formula managers. Now, we're asking them to do things that are right for their store, for their clientele, to take risks, to develop a climate in that store that has the customers coming back and ensures employee satisfaction.

The firm has changed its strategy to adopt a more decentralized management system and, at the same time, hired store managers who do not have in-store experience. This is at a time when top management is also likely not to have had in-store experience. Some store managers and employees feel that this change from store-trained to college-trained managers has led to a problem because college-trained managers do not know enough about store operations. One store manager described the change:

> You got to put yourself in the employee's position a lot of times. I don't think we [managers] do that a lot. That's why I can relate to these guys, because I've done their job. That's where we've got a problem with some college kids coming into management. They've never worked for a grocery store. I worked for X before I worked for SuperStores, as a bagger and checker, and as a stocker in the grocery department. When I was 16 till I got

out of college. I thought I had a lot going for me when I went into training over a lot of [management trainees].

Store size increased. Stores became increasingly differentiated. More managers were college educated rather than trained on the job. These factors combined to make it more difficult for managers to handle daily store operations. As Simon (1976) notes, rationality is limited by a manager's experience and sets of skills as well as by access to information. The problems of bounded rationality were becoming more apparent at SuperStores, because many of the operations in the store were outside the area of expertise of the store manager.

One additional factor that has contributed to the lack of store experience by managers is union work rules that prevent nonmembers (i.e., managers) from doing bargaining-unit work. The union has used its monopoly power to prevent substituting manager labor for clerk labor. This policy not only ensures that union members get the hours needed for this work but it also maintains the workers' monopoly over the skills required to do this work. The most extreme case of this monopolization in is the meat department:

Cutter: No one knows what goes on in the meat department. Not the managers, not the other grocery people. We want to keep it that way. We're a tough nut to crack. It's our own private world back there.

Q: Do the managers get trained in meat?

Cutter: They get a little, about three weeks.

Q: Do they learn to cut?

Cutter: Not really. They only scratch the surface. I tell them, "Do you want to cut? Here, here's a piece of meat. I'll turn on the saw for you and you can cut it. Then, I'll pick up your fingers for you and take you to the hospital so you can get them sewn on." I don't want some comanager cutting his fingers off in my department.[2]

While the other departments don't have quite this extreme of monopoly closure, the work rules still help them maintain their autonomy and may contribute to the decentralization of SuperStores. Montgomery (1979:13) notes that nineteenth-century craftsmen maintained their control over production by refusing to work in the presence of management. Thus, part of the political context of this organizational innovation is that an organized work force is better able to resist management centralization. Nonunion firms might find that it is easier for management to gain the knowledge necessary to centralize control.

The Problem of Local Demand

The problems of bounded rationality were even more obvious as chains grew larger. It became increasingly difficult for the central office to develop marketing plans that were appropriate for all the stores in the chain. Some stores were quite distant from the general office, or even from the division office. One store manager described his problems with the division office's marketing plans:

Q: Have you found better ways of doing things than "by the book"?

Store Manager: Yes. Getting items this particular area needs. I had one hell of a time trying to get chicken broth in a 46- or 52- ounce can. The [division] office computer says it don't sell, but in this town it does. I had to fight a lot of people to get some up here. I finally had to buy it directly from a warehouse in Town A who happened to have a truck up here. He dropped off 150 cases. My customers were driving me nuts so I had to get it. Mexican food. Chorizo. People are driving [across the state] for it. I found a way to get it here. Mexicans aren't the only ones who use it. People use it for seasoning. I found a vendor in [a nearby town], but he must have had cash-flow problems, 'cause he got out of it. So I went down to [a farther town] and found another person who's now bringing it in. I had to go out and do what I thought was best for [our town] versus what was the norm out of [division office].

The problem of matching product mix to local demand is particularly important in retail food. While one of the managers said that the advantages he could gain by his new freedom were generally minute (a few cents on a case of soda pop, for example), he felt these minute improvements added up. Since the net profit in retail food is generally about 1% of total sales (see Figures 2.2 and 2.3), these minute

Table 5.1. Supermarket Delis Containing Hot Food
        Cases, by Region

Regions	Percentage of Total Supermarkets
Northeast	34%
East Central	46
Southeast	84
West Central	53
Southwest	80
West Pacific	30
US Average	55%

Source: McLaughlin, German, and Uetz 1986:22.

advantages can mean the difference between a successful store and an unsuccessful store. Other national retailers had similar problems. Chandler (1962) describes the problems Sears had trying to maintain appropriate stock in a national chain of retail outlets (for example, sending snow skis to stores in the South and bathing suits to Minnesota in the winter). Its solution was adopting a multidivisional structure based on regional divisions. This structure was better able to match product mix with local demand.

This problem of local demand is particularly crucial for the new specialty shops. For example, while the grocery departments are fairly uniform across stores, the deli has to cater to local tastes, because it is closer to the end product, table food. As DeVault (1984) notes, the production of table food in the household is highly problematic because of the variety of individual tastes and the need to handle various contingencies (such as the need for different foods each meal). As firms begin to move into the production of table food, they also have to begin to anticipate the vagaries of this market, although in a more aggregate form. The particular mix of products sold in a deli is highly idiosyncratic. The mix varies by region, ethnicity, and class of clients (McLaughlin, German, and Uetz 1986, *PG* June 1975a, *PG* June 1982, *PG* October 1982). For example, in the South, most delis have barbecue and a hot table. In the Northeast, delis consist primarily of cold meats, cheeses, and salads (see Table

5.1). Because SuperStores covers a 20-state area, the problem of matching local demand to a central plan is particularly problematic.

Decentralization to the Shop Floor

SuperStores' one-stop-shopping strategy and its expansion strategy put it into new markets, both product and geographic. At the same time, the increase in store size and the increase in managers with little store experience created the potential for a set of in-store relations where no one had the necessary competence to carry out the day-to-day operations of the new strategies. To correct this problem, Super-Stores started a program of decentralizing decision making to the store level, giving workers a great deal of autonomy. They called this the "entrepreneurial store." A store manager described the change:

> Store Manager: In the last few months they've set up 5 stores in our marketing area as entrepreneurial stores, which we are one. That is we have the latitude to run the store independently. We still have the framework and guidelines of SuperStores to follow, but [before] any kind of sales came down to the store from the division office. You had a sales plan with little latitude a far as getting off of it. The new plan is we're able to contact suppliers directly. I met with two suppliers today where we're going out and setting up truckload sales on our own. Trying to create more excitement and being able to react to local competition and react faster. That's the biggest advantage.

> Q: Where was the source of this change?

> Store Manager: The division, although it had some input from the store. Going back in time, it's hard with 100–110 stores to come up with 110 plans that work. Consequently, you issue one master plan, sales plan or whatever, and say this is what works for the majority of the stores. With our store being located about 270 miles from [division office], everything is geared toward the [division office] market, yet our customers identify with [a different major city]. We were the first store to go on this program to be closer to what the customer wanted as far as promotions, new product, different items, which we needed to carry but which weren't carried by the stores in [division office]. This whole program allowed us to go out and get those items.

Thus, SuperStores recognized the problem of trying to run a centralized operation when faced with heterogeneous markets and attempted to counter the problem by setting up decentralized decision making through the entrepreneurial store. A central office (either the regional office or the general office) would recommend marketing plans for the stores, and the stores were then free to modify these plans within limits.[3] The management of SuperStores stated that such a structure would better allow the stores to adapt to local conditions: One division manager explained: "When you disperse decisionmaking, you're really freeing up the creative energy of an organization. By placing responsibility closer to the point of contact with the customer, you encourage employees to see the customer's needs without a whole lot of filters" (1986 Annual Report).

In addition, to accommodate the larger store size, SuperStores subdivided the grocery department (the largest department in the store), creating the new department head positions for frozen foods, dairy, and nonfoods (see Figure 1.2). Thus, some of the stockers who previously had specialized in a particular aisle or section were promoted to the position of department head for one of these subdepartments, with responsibility for ordering, stocking, maintaining, and supervising in their subdepartment. This change in job classification reflected the increased responsibility and competence required of these workers.

Thus, through a series of reorganizations, the firm has decentralized, first to the division level, then to the store manager level, and finally to the level of the hourly workers (the department heads and clerks). This new decentralized structure takes advantage not only of the large firm size to keep prices low through scale economies but also of worker knowledge to help the organization respond to the various demand contingencies in each store. This change is consistent with much of the current management literature on how to develop a successful firm in today's changing economy, which emphasizes flexible structures and the importance of encouraging employee input (Kanter 1983, Ouchi 1981, Peters and Waterman 1982). In fact, one of the store managers I interviewed asked that all of his department heads read Peters and Waterman's *In Search of Excellence*. The following sections explore how such a structure works in practice. In particular, I focus on the issues of worker skill, governance, employee training, and worker status.

Decentralization, Worker Autonomy, and Worker Skill

Some of the most obvious manifestations of the one-stop-shopping strategy are the new specialty shops. These new service departments are fairly large and complicated units within the stores. In a typical supermarket of around 80 employees, there are about 15 workers in the combination deli-bakery, with average sales of over $300,000 per year. In the new, larger stores of several hundred employees, there are about 50 workers in the deli-bakery, with annual sales of over $1 million (McLaughlin, German, and Uetz 1986). A deli-bakery accounts for approximately 6% of total sales.[4] In one store for which I have data (a smaller deli-bakery combo), the gross profit was 42% (in 1988), compared to 23% in the grocery department. Thus, this strategy was helping to solve the problem of the profit squeeze. The deli-bakery contributed 10% of the total store gross profit, about the same as the produce department, which had also become larger, as stores expanded their produce selections.

These deli-bakeries sell quite an array of goods. Delis sell cold lunchmeats and cheeses, as well as various prepared foods such as cold salads (potato, fruit, three-bean, pasta, chicken, shrimp) and side dishes (cole slaw, baked beans), fried or barbecued chicken, barbecued ribs, beef barbecue, meatballs, calzone, various Chinese dishes (fried rice, sweet and sour pork, egg rolls, and pot stickers), desserts (cannoli, cheese cake—with and without chocolate), fresh wursts, and pasta.[5] The exact mix varies considerably from store to store. The deli also provides catering services. It will cook (for take out) a traditional holiday meal for 8–10 people consisting of ham or turkey with gravy, dressing, potatoes, rolls, green beans, and apple pie. One store in my sample sold 160 of these $30 dinners on a recent Thanksgiving. The bakery sells fresh bread (sliced to order), bagels and rolls, pies, doughnuts, cookies, and cakes, decorated to order. At SuperStores, the deli-bakery workers prepare most of the hot foods and salads and bake most of the baked goods, either from scratch or using frozen dough. The service meat counter might carry such items as stuffed pork chops, chicken breasts stuffed with sausage and mozzarella, and shish kabob, as well as steaks, rolled roasts, and ground meat. McLaughlin, German, and Uetz (1986) conducted a survey of 31 supermarket firms and found that 63% of stores that served hot food had an equipped kitchen with which to prepare food in-store. Stores in the South and Midwest were even more likely to prepare food in-store (Table 5.1).

Some of the delis also include a restaurant, with a grill, serving hot sandwiches, hamburgers, and breakfasts.[6] In these cases the deli workers cook to order as well as making the prepared foods. These in-store restaurants are much like small, family restaurants. At one store in my sample, the restaurant had more than 40 items on the menu, in addition to drinks and desserts. There would often be a line to be seated for Sunday breakfast at the restaurant-deli, even with competition from several restaurants on the same commercial strip where it was located.

The decentralization of decision making allowed stores to match product mix to local demand. However, because store managers had little in-store experience, and in general, no experience in the specialty shops, they were not in a position make these decisions. Super-Stores solved the problem by having production in the stores and then giving store employees a great deal of autonomy. For example, in the deli the particular mix of products sold reflected the competence and tastes of the employees and their perceptions of demand at the store level as well as the central office's plans for implementing a marketing strategy. A deli worker described how her department determined its product mix:

Q: Have you got a grill there?

Deli Clerk: Yes, we've got everything, a grill, stove, oven, deep fryer. We make doughnuts, fried chicken. We have hot lunches. We can make whatever we want.

Q: Do you have recipes?

Deli Clerk: No, whoever works the morning just makes what she likes, what will sell. You try to make something simple, brats and sauerkraut, fried chicken, meat loaf. . . . You get two vegetables and a potato, or roll.

It's about $2.00. We sell out every day. When you're cooking, you decide what you want, and then take it off the shelves. You can make anything, because we have all the equipment and we have a whole grocery store. . . . We also make all our own salads. We make pasta salad, antipasto, potato salad, ambrosia, stuffed shells.

There is a great deal of worker autonomy at the store level. While the division office issues a marketing plan, the store employees have a lot of flexibility within that plan. Not all firms give this much production autonomy to their workers, and there has been debate in the trade publications concerning whether production should be done in-store or in central commissaries (*PG* June 1975a, *PG* May 1984). Given a bundle-of-tasks perspective, in-store production seems to make more sense for many types of foods. Because service work is intermittent, adding production tasks to the bundle allows workers to spend their downtime on production (*PG* May 1984). Not only is their labor used more efficiently but the complexity of the jobs also increases and therefore, presumably, job satisfaction increases (Mottaz 1985). Similarly, the move into catering allows the firm to diversify in a way that takes advantage of both the production skills of employees (who must be able to cook for in-store production) and the downtime in their schedule (because the meals can be made between waiting on customers during the morning and still be ready for an event that afternoon or evening) (*PG* May 1984). Employees of specialty shops can also use this time to prepare goods for self-serve, such as premade sandwiches or fresh pizzas. In-store production not only allows better time management by employees, it also allows a better fit to the variation in local demand, since employees know what sells in their market. Also, many firms do not sell enough of any given product in any marketing area to justify a central commissary for that marketing area (*PG* June 1975a). Finally, in-store preparation allows firms to take advantage of mistakes in other parts of the store. For example, the deli can run a special on meat loaf if the meat department grinds too much meat or make a Polynesian stir-fry if the produce department overorders pineapples. Thus, while interdependencies in the store are limited (the different departments are not forced to interact very often), there are synergies among the departments that can increase productivity or buffer the store from uncertainties.

Workers in other departments, including grocery, produce, and frozen foods, also described their jobs as having a great deal of autonomy under the new decentralized system.7 The following quote is typical:

Q: What are your duties?

Head Produce: I order produce. I also buy produce locally. I oversee all the display building. Oversee the other clerks. Everything in the department. Even the amount of profit. Everything is up to me now. I like that.

Q: What are you allowed to buy locally?

Head Produce: Starting this year, I can buy anything I want to buy. I do a lot of my own buying.

As store size increased, new departments were created with the responsibilities of stocking and ordering for a subsection of the grocery department. This ordering autonomy also extended in some cases to choice of vendors as well as to product mix. Even within the grocery department, stockers would often have responsibility for ordering for a particular set of aisles. As noted in Chapter 4, some of the problems of ordering include keeping track of and predicting seasonal fluctuations in demand; keeping track of holidays and stocking appropriate food and nonfood items, particularly for ethnic holidays, which may only be celebrated in certain stores in the city; and keeping track of special deals offered by vendors and calculating how to maximize the benefits of such deals. One of the department heads described how he manipulates inventories to increase his department's return:

Head Frozen Food: You just don't order for the next delivery. You have the freezer. You try to keep the freezer as empty as possible, because the freezer makes you money, because you can buy the merchandise when it's on sale and stick it back there. When it goes off sale, if you bought the right stuff, you can make a pile. Minute Maid orange juice. We had it for 89 cents, one week only. I ordered 200 cases. When it went off sale, I had it back up to $1.29. It took me 8 weeks to get rid of, but I made 600 dollars extra that 8 weeks.

By taking advantage of specials from the vendors, the department head can increase his earnings. But he has to balance the desire to fill his back room or freezer with sale merchandise with the requirement that he have enough back stock of the regular merchandise to keep from running out between orders. And if he overorders, he won't have storage facilities for the extra merchandise. Ordering and maintaining stock is particularly problematic in the perishables departments, which require a cooler or a freezer for their products (meat, deli, bakery, seafood, frozen food, dairy). When asked whether his job required more skill with decentralization, one department head described his new burdens as follows: "Yes. I have more responsibility. I didn't worry about anything when I went home when I was a stocker. I take on some of the responsibility that the managers have, a lot of things a normal stocker wouldn't have."

Thus, SuperStores has even managed to decentralize the worrying, traditionally one of the prerogatives of management. However, workers also expressed pride in their autonomy and responsibility. For example, when asked, "What is the most difficult part of your job?" one department head answered, "Keeping everything the way I want it. I take a lot of pride in my department. I want it perfect." Similarly, the above-quoted head of produce noted his satisfaction with his new autonomy, saying, "Everything is up to me now. I like that."

In addition to the problems of matching local demand, there is also the problem of handling irregularities in the production process (Perrow 1967). Because workers in the specialty shops were handling somewhat nonstandard inputs (foods), they had to be able to adjust production to fit the set of inputs they were using. The following two quotes illustrate some of the problems in food production:

Bakery Clerk: Usually we repair our own stuff if we can, rather than waste it. Sometimes our proofer doesn't give humidity. That's important. Otherwise the bread will be real dry. So, we just dump water on the floor of the proofer, until we can get it fixed. So, we've got our little ways.

Q: How long did it take for you to learn your job?

Head Deli: Real good? About a year. I made a mess of it when I first started. When I first started I was in charge of doughnuts. It was highly perishable. If you made some minor mistake, it could affect the product. I might ruin a whole screen full of doughnuts. I didn't have any really big losses, like a whole freezer full or something. We've had the doughnut fryer ever since I've been here, 13 years. That's what I started doing. Now, if I went back there, I probably couldn't do it, I've been away from it for so long.

The first quote from the bakery clerk points out the need for workers to adjust the production process to account for variations in the inputs, in this case the equipment (cf. Sabel 1982). The second quote describes the skill required to produce the product, as well as the perishability of the product (cf. Buchanan and Boddy 1983). These skills are similar to the skills required of floor workers in chemicals production (Halle 1984). As Halle notes, seemingly small (and undocumented) adjustments can have a substantial effect on product quality or production rate. The quote from the head deli also emphasizes that the job takes time to learn and that the skills must be practiced or they will atrophy. She also mentions one of the keys to the decentralization strategy, her significant seniority.

Finally, not only did these workers know what to prepare, how to prepare it, and how much to order, they also had to be able to handle customers. A recent survey of newspaper food editors found that dissatisfaction with uninformed employees in the perishables departments was the second-most frequent complaint they receive about food stores (*PG* January 1986b).[8] This suggests that worker competence was important to the success of these departments. In fact, increasing customer service was the major impetus for adopting the one-stop-shopping strategy.

One important component of customer service is teaching customers how to incorporate new products into their household economy (*PG* May 1984). Various department heads describe the importance of teaching customers.

Q: What are your job duties?

Head Seafood: One big demanding thing is that people aren't very knowledgeable. You have to explain what to do. They'll order seafood out, but when it comes to fixing it at home, they don't.

Q: Is your job skilled?

Head Produce: Yes. Not only do I have to be able to buy my produce, I have to be able to talk to the customers. I've got people who won't buy anything unless I ok it. This is a melon I like. A lot of time, when I'm building a display and I find an extra good melon, I'll put it to the side, so when customers come up, I'll say, "Hey, this is the one I was going to buy for myself."

Store Manager: It's important for service meat people to be trusted by the housewife, so she can ask for menu suggestions, the best buy of the week and so on. A service meat employee who has the confidence of his customers can be a tremendous salesman for the department. (*PG* May, 1984)

Thus, workers share their product knowledge with customers, which helps overcome customer reluctance to buying unfamiliar or variable products. The store manager above used older men in this role, because he felt they had both the product knowledge and the trust of the customers.

Not only did these departments require workers to be minimally competent in customer service, but, to be successful, workers had to get to know their customers (for example, what they liked and disliked and when they shopped). Over time, employees would build up a stock of store-specific knowledge that increased the profitability of the department. For example, employees would build a following: certain customers came to that store specifically to buy fish or sandwiches or cakes from that employee.

Q: Do service departments get a following?

Store Manager: They can. Our seafood shop is a good example. They meet the same people. They ask for them by name. They only want Bill or only want the meatcutter Duke to wait on them. It's because of the talking they do. You encourage that, sure. A lot depends of the department and the department head. Bill [head seafood] has encouraged his people to talk with customers. In the deli, we're kind of weak on that. We wait on the people, and say "Hi," but people don't come here just because we have a deli. . . . Certain departments are better than others. Seafood is probably the highest as far as sales, so it affects sales. Cheese, floral behind him.

While I could not get the data necessary to calculate this relationship, all the store managers I interviewed said there was a relationship between employee turnover and profitability in the specialty shops. While such attachment to the service provider is expected for doctors, lawyers, and other professionals and is common among waitresses, bartenders, and mechanics, it is interesting that it also occurs among such limited interactions as that between a grocery store employee and customer. The typical transaction is quite short. Yet, strong followings do develop. For example, customers would sometimes follow a favorite employee when that employee transferred to a neighboring store. These followings develop because even in a so-called routinized interaction, such as that between a cashier and a customer, the development of a client bond can reduce alienation for the employee. One checker, referring to her personal relations with customers, described her store as having a "family atmosphere." She felt a personal attachment to her customers, who regularly shopped during her shifts. The client bond can also reduce the friction that results from a breakdown in the routine. For example, a cashier who knows the customer might let her cash a check over the set amount; an office clerk might call a customer to tell her a check has bounced, rather than charge her the returned check fee; or a bagger might bag her groceries in the way she prefers without special direction. A client bond can also increase the speed of the interaction because the employee can use her knowledge to increase the efficiency of the interaction. For example, a deli clerk who knows a customer always comes in at a certain time for the same sandwich can have his order ready for him when he arrives.

There have been various accounts that claim that service work has been routinized, in large part to eliminate this relationship (Hochschild 1983, Leidner 1988). Professionals have the organizational power (e.g., the AMA for doctors) and the individual power (because they possess a rare and valued competence) to resist routinization (Freidson 1975). However, even among lower status service workers, there are countertendencies that work against routinization and alienation. The first is the desire to provide service that matches the needs of individual customers. The second is the desire to interact socially with others seen on a regular basis.

Thus, an employee's productivity in a service occupation is in large part determined by his or her relationship with clientele. Technical competence includes knowledge about his or her clientele, which he or she uses to encourage continued patronage. This competence is not easily transferred to new employees. The change in strategy in part also changed the relations between customers and workers. The new strategy brought the service relation back in to the store. Workers now had to have customer-service skills, and firm success under these new conditions would depend in part on the ability of workers to satisfy the new demands for service.

I asked one of SuperStores' corporate managers about the importance of a skilled work force. His response summarizes the firm's attitudes about the importance of worker skill:

Q: Does a successful store require a core of full-time people who are going to stay around a long time?

Corporate Manager: Absolutely. I think you need a core of solid citizens. There's some highly skilled people in our stores.

Q: In what ways are they skilled?

Corporate Manager: Somebody who's running a meat market or somebody who's running a produce market has perishable ordering. He has to understand perishable requirements. In produce they have 150 items. Everything from baked potatoes to highly perishable Chinese endive. He, or she, has to know how to prepare it, because customers want to know, "What is this and how do you prepare it?" They have to know how to take care of it. Customers want to know how to cook it, how to keep it. Meat, the same: everything from rock cornish hen through sea bass. "How do you cook it?" "How do I take care of it?" "When do I know it's good and not good?" "What spices do I use?" How to manage that inventory that's going to blow up on you or go bad in three days. Plus order enough to have it for high fluctuating sales days. Monday's the lowest sales day of the week; Saturday's the largest. How do you order product and get it ready to go out there and display it? Water it? Freeze it? Price it; identify it; tell your mother how to prepare it. I don't think high school kids can do that.

Q: This sounds like the department head's job.

Corporate Manager: There are several people who are full-time employees in each one of these departments. The customer doesn't come in and say, "Are you the department head?" A customer comes in and says, "Tell me about this." You can't have a rube standing there saying, "I don't know. Go see the department head." Plus we're open 24 hours at some of these locations.

Q: So you want to have 1 or 2 people on every shift.

Corporate Manager: You want somebody responsible for that department there all the time. Anybody who's on the floor has to know something about what they're selling.

The above quote emphasizes the importance of worker skill for SuperStores. This manager was arguing that the stores depend on worker skill, and not just among the department heads, but among all the full-time employees. He also points out the need for at least minimal competence among all employees, full-time and part-time, in order for the customer-service strategy to succeed. He notes that worker skills consist of production competence, ordering savvy, product knowledge, and customer service skills. Benton et al. (1991) note that, in general, service firms are moving toward increasing what Benton et al. call technical skill, conceptual skill, and communication skill, in order to stay competitive in the increasingly competitive markets of the 1990s.

This decentralization is possible because of the firm-specific skills that these workers have, in particular, their knowledge of local demand. We can use seniority as a proxy for knowledge of local conditions. The median seniority of United Food and Commercial Workers members (the union that represents grocery workers) is seven years (UFCW 1987). In my sample, the median seniority is six years. Thus, these workers had enough experience to have accumulated many store-specific skills, which the organization could tap in the decentralized structure model. In addition, workers in this firm were paid fairly well, which we can view as another proxy for the skill involved. This high pay is also a partial explanation for high seniority. For example, in 1985, in one of the divisions in the Midwest, the head grocery, head produce, and head front end in a large store each made $12.72 per hour, plus benefits.[9] The head meatcutter made $14.58 per hour. The head deli made $12.34 per hour. The deli and bakery clerks with full seniority (four or more years) made $7.85 or $8.90, depending on their hire date.[10] While wages are not a perfect proxy for skill (Beechey 1982), these wage levels do suggest that this work is more than simply unskilled labor and, combined with the other evidence, suggest that the firm is relying on a work force with more than a marginal amount of skill.

Worker-Management Committees

Like so many organizations during this period, SuperStores began to recognize the utility of regular avenues for worker input into management decision making (Cole 1985). The stores I observed had two forms of store meetings. First, there was a daily meeting of the department heads and store managers. In this meeting they discussed immediate concerns, such as how to implement an upcoming promotion. In addition, there were less frequent meetings between the store manager and the workers. Every month, there is also a longer meeting with the department heads. A store manager gave the agenda for the next meeting:

> Store Manager (during the daily meeting): I want each of you [department heads] to take a turn giving a presentation about a new item or special you're promoting. For example, Tom [head frozen food] claims he's got a pretty good pizza. You cook up a couple and we'll try it, to see if it's any good. Jan and Becky [head, cheese department, and head deli, who make fresh pizzas] are going to be your toughest critics. Then I want us all to promote the stuff. Let customers know these things are here.

In addition, at least every other month there is a meeting of the advisory board, a committee made up of nondepartment head representatives from all the departments. They meet with the store manager and discuss work-related issues, such as morale problems and disputes over scheduling. These meetings serve the dual function of improving performance by generating ideas and spreading them across departments and increasing worker satisfaction by allowing workers to air grievances and contribute to management decision making.

Problems with the New Structure

The previous sections describe the changes in work that resulted from the adoption of the decentralized structure. However, such a reorganization of the division of labor creates several problems for the organization. First, there is the problem of control, the governance problem discussed by Williamson (1975). With a largely autonomous work force, it is more difficult for the organization to ensure that employees direct their energies toward advancing the organization's goals. Second, it is more challenging to find or create workers with the necessary competences to handle the various tasks required by the new structure. One solution is to encourage workers to spend a long time with the firm so they will acquire sufficient firm-specific knowledge. This section will deal with how workers acquire that knowledge. Finally, there is the question of worker skill and worker pay. Have these workers been able to translate their autonomy and skill into higher pay? The last part of this section addresses this issue.

Worker Control: Preventing Opportunism

A decentralized organization must determine how to control its work force (Williamson 1975). In small, autonomous workshops, governance is through the market. Large, centralized firms control workers through bureaucratic rules (Edwards 1979). Large, decentralized firms need a structure of internal governance to prevent opportunism. Chandler's analysis of the multidivisional form suggests that decentralized firms could maintain control over the work force through statistical controls. By keeping track of outputs and comparing productivity across like units, managers can see if the unit is operating efficiently, without delineating and supervising the daily tasks of the work force (Child 1977, ch. 6). In this sense statistical controls differ from bureaucratic control. Edwards, describing bureaucratic control, says, "The main concern seems to be not measuring output, but instead checking compliance with the rules" (1979:140). In a large, decentralized firm, in contrast, managers do not specify how the work is to be done, they only require that it be done efficiently. This type of control requires measuring output in some meaningful way. Workers on an assembly line, for example, cannot be easily evaluated in this way, since the productivity of one worker is highly dependent on the productivity of all the workers. Statistical control requires some independence of workers, or at least small work units, to allow some reasonable way to measure output.[11]

Such a system also requires a countable product. In retailing, sales works nicely as a metric, and sales volume was one of the main criteria by which SuperStores evaluated departments (and department heads). This system also requires comparable units in order to determine if the department is doing as well as can be expected, which makes statistical controls more suitable for large firms. For example, SuperStores would evaluate a produce department by comparing it to other produce departments in the division, perhaps controlling for size of store and type of neighborhood. All firms can use historical comparisons as the basis for statistical controls. However, this method does not take into account factors, such as business cycles, that cause performance to decline independent of internal factors.

The decentralized structure leaves the firm exposed to the threat of opportunism by the skilled workers. Workers under such a system could easily goldbrick or pilfer from the company. Since managers are responsible for many workers in several departments and do not have detailed knowledge of the production process, they cannot supervise either by direct control or by bureaucratic control. Instead, SuperStores relies on a system of statistical controls: measuring inputs and outputs, without specifying the transformation process. Lawrence (1958) and others (Chandler 1962, Child 1977, Gyllenhammar 1977) have noted that statistical controls are an effective means of supervising workers when their work cannot be supervised directly.

Workers also have an incentive to direct their energies to company goals if they are part owners of the company. Rosen (1991) found that employee-owned firms performed slightly better than similar, non-employee-owned firms. However, when employee-owners had an opportunity to participate in organization decisions, these firms performed substantially better. Similarly, Cotton et al. (1988) found that unless participation is tied to ownership, or to a similar reward structure, it tends to be short-lived and ineffective.[12] SuperStores does have a strong employee ownership program (over 25% of the company stock is employee owned). In addition, some stores in the company have also incorporated bonuses into the incentive system. However, none of my respondents mentioned their ownership stake or bonuses as an incentive for them to participate and increase performance. Rather, employees seemed to participate because of the autonomy and responsibility they had been given under the decentralized structure. As Cotton et al. (1988) point out, successful employee-participation programs give employees a real say in their work group. Organizations that give workers only nominal input often find that workers quickly withdraw their participation.

At the store level, the solution to the problems of how to implement the new strategy, particularly in the service departments, is left to the department head or even the clerks. Workers have a great deal of autonomy in the particulars of the process. Managers make the department head responsible for the performance of the department and leave the details of production to the department head and other workers. In many ways, the department heads are the equivalent of the store managers in the older, conventional stores. They are promoted through the ranks and are primarily concerned with daily operations decisions for their departments. When I asked a store manager how department heads are evaluated, he answered: "Through me. Sales, gross profit, conditions, product quality. I evaluate them the same as I get evaluated. I believe they are management people in their own department. If we're going to perform as a store, each department has to perform."

The department head is responsible for the whole department. SuperStores evaluates the department head on her department's performance with respect to individually negotiated goals based on the previous year's performance and the performance of other comparable departments (cf. Lawrence 1958). If the department head does not keep up to par, she can be demoted. Since the department head has come up through the ranks (unlike the store manager) and since she works on the shop floor, she is in a position to direct employee training and daily operations. The departments are under a sort of budgetary subcontracting system. Some department heads described their jobs as like running their own business.

Q: Is your job skilled?

Head Deli: Yes. Over the years it's taken a long time to learn everything. You're like your own businessperson. You're running the department as if it were your own business. You're responsible for everything in it. Even though it's not my money, I'm still responsible for it.

The department head has almost total autonomy within her department (including hiring responsibility), provided that her rates of return are in line with the departments in other stores.[13] Thus, by creating semiautonomous departments within the store and by making the department head responsible for the department, the firm can reduce opportunism by threatening to sanction the department head. SuperStores has not taken decentralization to the extreme found, for example, among miners in the Tavistock studies, where self-selected teams of workers were paid a collective piece rate and wages were divided according to agreements made within each team (Trist et al. 1963). Workers at SuperStores were still paid primarily by an hourly wage (with some stores beginning to institute bonus systems). Still, departments had substantial autonomy within the stores.

The department head is a merging of the roles of manager and worker. The blending of these roles is one of the keys to successful decentralization. Firms with sharply divided management and labor ranks are less likely to achieve the cooperation needed for decentralization to be successful.

One reason for the high degree of autonomy in the departments is that there is relatively low interdependence among the departments (Thompson 1967). Each department is more like a separate shop. There is some interdependence (for example, between the bakery and the deli), but even there the units are loosely coupled (Scott 1987). Trist et al. (1963) note that this is an important precondition for setting up autonomous work group. The interdependencies that do exist are reflected in the structure, as Thompson (1967) would suggest. For example, the deli and the bakery have a common head, and the dairy, frozen food, and grocery all have a common head. For the most part, however, there is little need to coordinate the outputs and inputs of the different departments, so there is little need to structure their activities externally. This suggests that decentralized structures are more suited for firms that are not highly interdependent. Retailing (both food and nonfood) is one example (see also Katz 1987). On the other hand, when the outputs of one work group are the inputs for another (such as product development in the auto industry [Clark et al. 1987]), then decentralized structures require more elaborate coordination mechanisms than those that were found in SuperStores (cf. Lawrence and Lorsch 1967).

Creating and Maintaining a Competent Work Force

The analysis of the decentralized structure at SuperStores shows the increased competence required of these new workers. It also shows the idiosyncratic patterns of growth in these departments. The product mix of a particular deli varies store by store within a given chain and depends heavily on the particular competences of the workers in that store. At the store level, the solution to the problems of how to implement the new strategy is left to the department head or clerks. The retail food chains have initiated a set of highly decentralized, autonomous subunits for producing and selling table food.

Upper management is not completely ignorant of store operations; people in those positions do provide each store with basic operations information (e.g., a sales plan) that would be sufficient to run a store. However, management recognizes (as the quotes in the beginning of the chapter show) that such plans are not enough to make a store maximally profitable. To maximize profit, or even to stay competitive, firms must rely on local expertise and local initiative. The decentralized structure is an attempt to harness local expertise and encourage local initiative.

In addition to production competence, workers in these departments also need customer-service skills, both general and specific. Because customers often evaluate service departments by their experience with the clerk, the clerks must be trained to interact successfully in order for the department to be profitable. A deli executive emphasized the training problem in service departments: High turnover as a result of using part-time workers "means a constant threat of inexperience and lack of salesmanship in an area where over-the-counter selling and knowledge of product is basic to building business and satisfying the customer. Training and giving part-timers some motivation to do a good job are persistent problems" (*PG* June 1983).

This deli executive emphasizes the importance of having workers with customer-service skills and the difficulty of reproducing those skills in the work force, particularly if there is high turnover.

The success of these autonomous departments depends heavily on the competence of the work force. Every manager interviewed noted the importance of training to the success of the new structure.

Benton et al. (1991) note that employee training is the key to competitiveness in the modern service sector. However, getting and maintaining a competent work force is problematic (More 1980). While previous studies have tended to concentrate on either the mass production model or the craft model of reproducing worker skills (Montgomery 1979, More 1980, Piore and Sabel 1984), neither of these models seems to be operating in the specialty shops. The training process in the specialty shops is a hybrid of these two models.

In the specialty shops, workers learn by starting with relatively simple, low-status tasks, such as staffing the counter (More 1980). They are given few or no production duties to start. For the first several weeks, they are always supervised. Whenever they have a problem, they are able to, and are expected to, ask a more senior employee for assistance. Over time, workers will be given more production jobs and more autonomy. Each additional task in the worker's bundle increases her informal status in the shop.

Which particular tasks a certain worker learns is not formalized but is determined by where there are openings at the time the worker is ready to progress and who is available to teach them the tasks that are part of that bundle. A department head describes her training program:

Q: How did you learn to be head seafood?

Head Seafood: Mostly by watching the people that had more seniority. Take over more responsibility. When people went on vacation, you were put in their position for a week's time. A lot of times you'd have to ask them to show you different things like the paperwork. They would take you aside and show you. If you don't get on them to show you, they don't ever show you. Mostly observing and then having them show you different things.

The tasks learned depend on who is available, opportunities presented by absences, and how aggressive the worker is in asking for training. It points to the lack of formalization of the training process. The following exchange reinforces that point: "A customer ordered a sandwich from the older, female worker in the deli. A young, male, deli clerk asked what she was doing. She said, 'Making a sandwich. Watch, then you'll know how to do it.' He said, 'I never made one for a customer before. I'd be afraid I'd screw it up. I had to write "Happy Birthday" on a cake last night. No one else was here. It looked pretty bad, but the lady liked it, so I guess it was OK.'"

The hard part about making a deli sandwich is not how to assemble the sandwich but rather how to price it. In my observations, I noted that sometimes the worker would charge a fixed price for the sandwich (and use some uncertain amount of ingredients), sometimes she would weigh the meat and charge by weight, possibly adding some fixed price for the condiments and other ingredients, sometimes she would weigh the whole sandwich and charge either the cost of the meat or some fixed cost per pound. While every store probably has some policy on this, I found little agreement in practice. Clerks who did not know the correct pricing would ask the other clerks on duty, who would offer some answer, although the answer was often not authoritative (for example, "I don't know. I usually just charge $2.29"). Thus, the informal practices of that store are reproduced through this word-of-mouth training. This example, as well as the one above, show the informal nature of much of the training.

An important characteristic of this system is that it must allow for worker interaction. For example, studies have noted that one of the problems with an assembly line is that it does not allow for worker interaction (Walker and Guest 1952). Walker and Guest note that assembly-line production prevents workers from learning the tasks in other parts of the production process because workers are not free to move around and observe others at work. Also, the noise level in many factories makes it difficult for workers to explain things to each other.

While management may discourage worker interaction with rules that discourage conversation because they feel it reduces productivity, such interaction is often the source of worker training. In the specialty shops, counter workers can generally see into the back room where production takes place, and they can move back and forth between the back room and the counter. Also, the noise level is fairly low, so workers can easily talk to one another. Thus, the physical layout of the specialty shops allows for worker interaction, thereby facilitating the informal training that the shops depend on. There are also more formalized channels of worker interaction, the various store meetings, which help spread worker knowledge within the store, particularly across departments. Formal training seminars help to spread information across stores, overcoming the isolation caused by the geographic dispersion of and lack of interaction among employees in different stores.

The result of this informal training scheme is that no two workers in the department necessarily have the same set of competences. Certain bundles of tasks have formal titles (and premium pay) attached. For example, responsibility for ordering generally falls on the department heads or their assistants. However, most workers are classified under one title—clerk (with some separation by department: grocery, deli-bakery, meat, nonfoods). This makes the job of scheduling especially difficult because the department head (who makes the schedule) must be able to distinguish among the various sets of competences that are subsumed under the title of, for example, deli clerk in order to match competences with required tasks for each shift. For example, only some of the workers will know how to open the store or department in the morning, while only some others will know how to close it at night. In addition, there is no mechanism that guarantees that every task will be covered by someone. Often, when someone quits, her competence is lost to the organization, and the other workers must try to re-create the competence on their own.

Formal Training

The training process at SuperStores is not completely haphazard. Because of the importance of worker skill, SuperStores has instituted a variety of formal training programs (Benton et al. 1991, ch. 4, discusses formal training in other retailing firms). For example, SuperStores had a set of training films and manuals that new workers were supposed to use.

> Corporate Manager: We spend millions of dollars training people. Training new hires, training head produce clerks how to train their people, information slide programs, video programs, how to prepare anything. Deli department. New sales techniques. How to make a Bavarian cream pie. How to ice a cake. We've got probably 85 Fairchild tapes on everything from how to keep rats out of your store and how to detect rodent

Table 5.2. Responses to the Question: "How Did You Learn to Do Your Job?" (Open Ended)

Response	Number
In-Store Training[1]	23
Picked It Up[2]	19
Outside Training[3]	13
Previous Experience[4]	8
Manuals[5]	3
Total Responses[6]	66

[1]One-on-one training from senior worker. "Other workers taught me." Includes apprenticeships.
[2]"I picked it up as I went along." "Trial and error."
[3]Training seminars, schools, or outside consultants/trainers.
[4]"I worked as X in previous jobs." "My family owned a grocery."
[5]Manuals, books, films.
[6]Total respondents, 51. Some responses fit more than one category and so were coded in all applicable categories.

problems all the way through how to say "Happy Birthday" on a birthday cake, all collected over a long time.

However, when asked how they learned to do their job, only 3 out of 51 respondents (6%) mentioned the training films or manuals, and none of those 3 mentioned them as their primary means of learning (see Table 5.2).

In addition to the packaged training materials, there are training seminars in production and customer service. These training sessions, which often require travel, consist of seminars by outside experts in marketing, production, or customer interaction, and also sessions for exchanging ideas among workers from the different stores. Management uses the training sessions as a mechanism for ensuring some minimal standards of competence, at least for department heads (who generally attend the training sessions), as well as for transmitting worker knowledge across the barriers of the autonomous, relatively isolated departments. Twenty-five percent of respondents said they had been given some sort of outside training

(Table 5.2). SuperStores sent many of its service people to a training seminar in order to teach them the skills of customer interaction (primarily how to handle customers who were agitated) (see Chapter 3). Thus, this firm at least has determined that the payoff in terms of increased sales is worth the cost of formally training its employees in customer-service skills. There are also training programs to increase marketing and production skills. One cheese shop head described the utility of these conferences:

Q: How did you learn to do your job?

Head, Cheese Department: I was taught by the previous cheese shop hostess. I've been to several seminars since I took over. I learned an awful lot. Every year there's one for promotions and selling. The last one I went to was for different types of cheese, explaining the different ways of cutting cheese. There's a lot I didn't know before. One was in Bloomington, one in Peoria. Next week I'm going to St. Louis for three days for what they're calling a foodfest. There'll be workshops for cheese shops for making Christmas baskets and all of our Christmas ordering. I'm dying to go. Then you bring that back and show your girls.

This department head explained that seminars were regularly given (annually for the promotion and selling seminar). She also noted her role in the firm's training program. The department head goes to the seminar and then comes back to train her clerks.

Managers also collected recipes (primarily by polling workers in different stores) and then published them for distribution among the stores (*PG* June 1981). These books represent the collective knowledge of the workers in the various stores. This approach could be considered a very crude form of Taylorism—extracting worker knowledge and concentrating it in the management role. But, workers were given this knowledge as a whole, rather than learning only a detailed aspect of the work, as Taylor suggested (Taylor 1911).

These training sessions and manuals did not eliminate worker autonomy or knowledge but rather expanded it by overcoming the structural constraint to worker interaction. This cooperation among workers, organized by management, is similar to the industrial districts of Sheffield and Lyons described by Piore and Sabel (1984). The variation in demand made the industrial district strategy, based on small shops with skilled, flexible work forces, more successful than mass production. While deli and bakery clerks are not as skilled as Sheffield cutlerers or Lyons silk makers, the deli and bakery workers do have considerable skill. And, like the cutlerers and silk makers, the deli clerks have to be flexible and able to deal with a changing and idiosyncratic demand.

But these specialty shops are much more isolated than the shops of the industrial districts. The movement of people and goods between the shops of the industrial district was one of the primary means of spreading the innovations that made the districts competitive with mass production. The training seminars and manuals are an attempt by the supermarkets to achieve the same goal of spreading ideas and techniques across the barriers of what are fairly isolated shops.

THUS, THERE WAS no rationalized training program (or more correctly, what rationality the training program had was overshadowed by informal aspects), nor was there a craft apprenticeship, to pass on the necessary competences required in the service departments. Rather, workers would try to learn what they could from observing and asking senior workers for help. SuperStores tried to facilitate this training by expanding the base of knowledge available to the workers. However, it still appears that most workers learn their jobs through experience and observing senior workers and that the range of competence varies considerably across workers. This lack of rationalization in the training process reflects the lack of specificity in the theory of the shop-floor implementation of the firm's one-stop-shopping strategy. I would argue that one side effect of a decentralized structure of responsible autonomy is that workers are often left on their own to learn skills where they can. Management facilitates skill acquisition with manuals and seminars, but the majority of skills is learned from informal interactions in the shops.

Thus, the new strategy put the firm into a more varied and unfamiliar market. The firm responded by reorganizing the relations in production to give workers more autonomy in order to take advantage of worker knowledge. However, reproducing that knowledge is problematic. This section showed how the new organization managed to create the in-store and cross-store relations that would transmit this knowledge to new workers and reproduce the decentralized structure.

Despite this slack in the training system, the organization on the whole has been successful. As Table 1.2 shows, there has been tremendous growth in the number of these departments, and they have been around now for quite some time. These departments have been successful not in spite of lack of management control but because of the lack of management control. The variability of local demand requires organizations to be flexible enough to respond to this demand. By leaving operating and training decisions to the workers, the organization has the flexibility it needs to succeed. The department head is charged with limiting opportunism.

Worker Skill, Status, and Pay

I have shown that the new structure in SuperStores (and at other firms in the industry) led to the creation of a relatively skilled and autonomous work force. From the point of view of the bundle of tasks, this change suggests that the deskilling thesis is not applicable to this case. However, skill is more than simply the level of competence required for a job. It also includes the scarcity and the status of the tasks involved (Beechey 1982, Walsh 1989). Have these workers been able to translate their competence into higher status, in terms of pay, for example? I will show that for the most part they have not been able to do so, because of the gender composition of these new jobs and because of the relative status of the tasks involved in these new departments.

As noted in Chapter 1, while the grocery industry is approximately 50% female, the sex distribution is highly skewed by occupation. The departments with the highest percentage of women are all service departments (deli, front-end checkers, and seafood). For the meat department, the women are all wrappers, a service occupation. On the other hand, the cutters, stockers, and produce workers are overwhelmingly male. While many of the service departments require skills that are not found in the other clerks, this work is often undervalued. Female workers are expected to enter the job with a bundle of competences: the ability to cook, the ability to identify foods (different fruits, for example), cleaning skills, and personal interaction skills (how to treat customers pleasantly, under any conditions). Managers assume that women have acquired these competences during their socialization into the role of adult female.

For example, in the deli-bakery, the necessary competence—knowing how to cook—is considered common sense, especially for women. Workers in the deli are primarily female. Managers assume that by hiring females, they will get the technical competence they need at a fairly low cost. McLaughlin, German, and Uetz of Cornell University, in their report on the economics of delis, estimate that 90% of deli heads are women. They explain this high number as follows: "First, the historically part-time status of deli staffs coupled with relatively low wage structures are not likely to attract male employees who are more apt to be in search of full-time employment. Moreover, the cooking and preparation-type duties typically involved in working in a deli are likely to be more familiar, at least historically, to women" (McLaughlin et al. 1986:11). Similarly, an article in *Progressive Grocer* noted that most firms use women in their delis because of women's better rapport with customers, better housekeeping skills, and greater interest in food preparation and service (*PG* June 1975a). Having deli workers cook allows management to coopt the knowledge female workers are presumed to have because of their training as consumers and household managers. Although the deli workers have quite a bit of technical competence, they have been unable to translate that competence into status honor, in part because of the perceived lack of scarcity of the competence. In addition as previous studies have shown, "women's work" in general has been undervalued (Cockburn 1987, Daniels 1988).

A similar change took place when SuperStores moved its produce scales from the produce department to the front end, in order to tie them directly to the computerized registers. In 1980, 26% of stores had the scale at the front end (*PG* February 1980). Produce workers have the competence of being able to identify the various types of produce, as well as knowing the lookup code for each. This competence is not trivial, given the increased size of the produce department (cf. *PG* February 1980, *PG* December 1983, *Time* August 11, 1986). While most people can tell an apple from an orange, they may not be able to tell a Red Delicious apple from a MacIntosh apple or to be able to identify some of the more exotic forms of produce. Having scales in the produce department, however, forced customers to wait in two lines, one at the scale, one at the checkout. This was a major violation of the service strategy—long lines at the checkout being the number one customer complaint. SuperStores moved scales to the front end. Firms assume that by having women working as checkers, their shopping experience would enable them to correctly identify the produce.

Q: Do you have any trouble identifying produce?

Checker: They had a session when they got the scanners where they taught us. I think it would be difficult for, say, teenagers who haven't cooked, who don't know. If you know pretty much, if you do a lot of cooking, you should pretty much know the stuff. But there are some things. A lot of new fruits. Star fruit, different things which come in. You ask if you're not sure. Either ask another checker or call the produce department and have them identify it for you.

The checker notes that there is some increase in the competence required for checkers. However, the assumption by management as well as checkers is that the mostly female checkers will know the different fruits and vegetables because of their experience as consumers. The checker does note that younger checkers will have more trouble because they do not have the necessary experience as consumers. Thus, management coopts the "common sense" knowledge of the work force and uses this knowledge to increase customer service and productivity, since the checker now weighs the produce as well as checks.

The following exchange suggests that such an assumption was optimistic. During my observations, I saw a checker who was unable to identify a piece of fruit (she couldn't tell if it was an expensive citrus fruit, which sold for $3.99 per pound, or an inexpensive orange, which sold for 79¢ per pound). She asked the checker in the next lane, who told her what it was and what the code number was. After the customer left, the second checker told the first, "I almost always pick the lower price code because most customers don't buy the expensive, exotic produce." This example shows how checkers use their knowledge of customer buying habits to help increase productivity on the front end (by saving the time to send a bagger to produce to get the correct price). It also shows that mistakes can be costly (as the above price difference illustrates). Thus, worker competence in this case is not trivial and cannot be assumed to be synonymous with gender.

To test the assertion that service jobs are undervalued and that this undervaluing is due to the gender mix of those jobs, I collected data on wages for the various occupational classifications for one union local, which included the workers in SuperStores, and included both meat and grocery workers. There were 30 occupations in the last contract (signed in 1987). The unit of analysis is the job classification, not incumbents. The N is the universe of store-level job categories for this firm in this city (excluding pharmacists and managers). For each occupation, I coded the hourly wage (1987 dollars), [WAGE], whether it was a service occupation, [SERVICE], whether it was predominantly male, female or mixed, [SEX], whether it was in the meat division, [MEAT], and whether it was a department head classification, [HEAD]. Being in the meat department and being a department head are two controls for the skill requirements of the occupation, with department heads being more skilled than clerks and meat workers more skilled than grocery. In addition, all workers are unionized and work for the same firm, in the same industry, and in the same city, so those sources of variance in wages are controlled. All wages are the top wage rate for each classification, to control for seniority. Thus, most of the variables that might explain differences in wage rates are either held constant or controlled for statistically.

I tested the following model: that female jobs are paid less than other jobs, even after controlling for skill (measured by being in the meat division or a department head). I ran an ordinary least squares (OLS) regression of WAGE on a CONSTANT, SEX, MEAT, and HEAD (see Table 5.3). The results (Model 1) show that female jobs are significantly lower paying than male jobs. The regression coefficients can be interpreted as the change in hourly wage, given a change in status. Thus, on average, female jobs pay a little more than $2.00 per hour less than comparable male jobs.

Table 5.3. Regression of Wages in Supermarkets
(Standard Errors in Parentheses)

Independent Variables	Model 1	Model 2
MEAT	0.542	1.141*
	(0.674)	(0.626)
HEAD	2.520***	2.058***
	(0.708)	(0.641)
SEX	−2.018**	−.610
	(0.788)	(0.840)
SERVICE		−2.410***
		(0.816)
CONSTANT	9.711	10.127
R^2	.519	.643
Adjusted R^2	.463	.586
N	30	30

*p<.10,   **p<.05,   ***p<.01

MEAT-1 if job is in meat department (includes deli, bakery and seafood), 0 otherwise.

HEAD-1 if job is a department head or assistant, 0 otherwise.

SERVICE-1 if service job, 0 otherwise.

SEX-1 if primarily a female job, 0.5 if mixed job, 0 if primarily a male job.

I then added SERVICE, to see if the effect of gender dropped out when controlling for service. As the results show (Model 2), female jobs are still lower paid than male jobs. However, the gender variable is no longer significant. Now, SERVICE has the largest impact. Service jobs pay $2.41 less per hour than comparable jobs that are not service (production and stocking jobs). In addition, MEAT is now significant, because the meat department includes a large number of low-paying service jobs in the deli, bakery, and seafood shops. After these jobs are partialed out, it becomes apparent that workers in the meat department earn significantly higher wages. This second model fit significantly better than the first ($F_{1,25}=6.72$, $p<.05$).

These results suggest that female-typed jobs are undervalued and that this undervaluing is due in large part to the service component of those jobs. This undervaluing of service workers is consistent with much of the feminist literature showing that female occupations are routinely devalued because they are female (Cockburn 1987, Daniels 1988, DeVault 1984, Jolly, Grimm, and Wozniak 1990, Kraft 1979, Pfeffer and Ross 1990). An important component of their competence is social interaction skills, which are important for productivity but not necessarily valued (Hochschild 1983). The following excerpt from an interview by *Progressive Grocer* with a management representative shows management's perspective on the value of feminine tasks.

> Q: Compared to other business or manufacturing, is there anything special about supermarket working conditions and requirements that should boost supermarket workers' wages over other workers?
>
> Management Representative: No, none. As a matter of fact, if anything it's to the contrary. The job in supermarkets or grocery warehouses from the standpoint of working conditions is a better job than a General Motors production line or a meat packing plant or a rubber factory. Sure there are onerous jobs in the supermarket industry, but by and large, compared to industrial jobs, the answer is no.
>
> Q: Some would point to the importance of employees being courteous, meeting with the public, treating the customer right, that more initiative is required as compared to a factory production line.
>
> Management Representative: What kind of stuff is that? Sure we demand checkers to be courteous and pleasant, but for Pete's sake, that's just as you would expect any human being to be courteous and pleasant. How much of an onerous demand is that? The checker, for instance, smiles and says good morning to the customers as they file past. No big deal. That's an imposition? (*PG* April 1976)

As Hochschild (1983) points out, the self-management required to appear "courteous and pleasant" independent of one's actual state, is, in fact, quite onerous, particularly in the long term.

The results of the regression shown in Table 5.3 reflect this attitude that feminine skills are not valuable. On the other hand, the fact that SuperStores is now training employees, including male meatcutters, to "be nice" suggests that companies are beginning to recognize the importance of these skills, even if they are feminine (see Chapter 3). The fact that the competences of these service workers, although important for the success of the department, are considered low status (common sense) hinders service workers' abilities to translate their competence into high status. This is an example of the importance of cultural perceptions in determining the "skill" of a job. While these workers are technically competent, they do not have a valued competence. I cannot tell from this analysis whether service skills are devalued because they are feminine or if females are devalued because they are doing service work. There is some research that suggests that the gender component is the dominant characteristic. For example, Pfeffer and Ross (1990) found that as jobs change from male to female, their compensation is reduced. Similarly, Thomas (1985) notes that by hiring low-status workers for a set of tasks, those tasks can be successfully undervalued, despite the competence required. He uses the case of lettuce cutters, who were largely undocumented immigrants. These workers were unable to translate their skills in cutting lettuce into higher pay or more job security.

While the workers in the specialty shops have many of the attributes of craft workers, such as flexible training and high autonomy, they have been unable to develop a craft organization or culture. While they are unionized, they are in an industrial union that is dominated by the meatcutters and grocery clerks. Because their competence is not scarce, because of the isolation of these shops, and because of the high opportunity costs of separating from their current union, it is difficult for the deli and bakery employees to develop the basis for a craft organization. In addition, because many of these workers are women, managers can successfully undervalue their competences, calling them common sense. Because of these factors, it is likely that management will be able to continue its strategy of depending on worker competence without having to pay for that competence. This organization has been able to take advantage of the existing status hierarchy to expand into new areas that, while requiring competent workers, can be filled by low-status workers who have those competences or can be trained for them (cf. Thomas 1985). This is an example of the importance of cultural factors in determining the outcome of the innovation. As Thomas (1985) notes, worker rewards are the result of complex interactions between the organization and technology of production and the status characteristics of the workers (mediated by the power of firms and actions by the citizenry and the state). While such a change in supermarkets could have led to the creation of a craftlike division of labor, the fact that these positions were staffed by low-status workers, and the fact that these tasks are devalued, led instead to the creation of a decentralized structure staffed with nominally low-skilled workers.

Summary

This chapter traces the implementation of the decentralized structure. Like the innovations described in the previous chapters, this change was problematic. It required regenerating the relations in production to accommodate the new sets of tasks and the new environmental contingencies the firm would be facing as a result of the expansion and diversification strategies. Such changes created problems of control, problems of training, and problems of worker status. There was little resistance to these changes on the part of the workers, since the changes added core tasks to their bundle, and many of these tasks (such as ordering) were high-status tasks. Customers also embraced the changes, since the old products were all available largely unchanged (it did take longer to get through the bigger store).

There has been extensive discussion in the management literature on the importance of increasing worker participation as a key to success. SuperStores has adopted such a structure, as this chapter has shown. While this structure has contributed to the firm's success (see Figure 2.3), it has also raised some important issues in terms of the labor process in a decentralized organization. In particular, I have pointed out that while such a structure is dependent on worker competence, management's withdrawal from the shop floor can lead to the neglect of the development of that competence. Workers did seem to learn a variety of skills during their tenure, but it is not clear if they had all the skills they needed to maximize their department's performance.

In addition, this chapter also shows that worker competence does not necessarily translate into worker status. Worker status is a function of the status of the incumbents of a job, as well as the technical competence required of those incumbents. This finding emphasizes

the importance of cultural factors, not just on the demand side (resulting from the increased number of women working or from
changes in eating habits) but also in the supply side (in terms of the
relative status of various tasks). By diversifying into services, Super-
Stores was able not only to fill the increased demand for service but
also to do so with relatively low-paid (female) workers.

Finally, it is possible that the autonomy and lack of routinization
observed in the stores was the result of newness and that as these
innovations matured, they would become more routinized (Stinchcombe 1990, ch. 5; Whyte 1961). The evidence suggests, however, that
this decentralized structure is a stable form. The main evidence is
that SuperStores began the decentralization to the store level 30 years
ago. In addition, stores are becoming more decentralized as units
become more diversified. If SuperStores modified its strategy to sell
more of the same product, we would likely see a move toward routinization. However, as long as the strategy continues to be increasing
the variety of products sold in ever larger stores spread over a wider
area, this firm is likely to maintain the decentralized structure.

6

CONCLUSION

THIS BOOK BEGAN with a comparison of the supermarket of the 1950s with the supermarket of the 1980s. We saw that these organizations have changed dramatically during this period. These changes prompted the following questions: what causes these changes and how have these changes affected the work of supermarket employees?

To answer these questions, I combined organization theory and labor process theory to develop a new model of innovation: the politicized context model. This model emphasized the importance of both environment (including technological changes, environmental uncertainty and munificence, and the cultural context) and politics. It also focused attention on the importance of the web of relations in production, both those inside the firm (workers and managers) and those with external actors (such as suppliers and customers). Innovations disrupt the existing sets of routines in the organization, and a successful innovation has to rebuild those routines in a way that is acceptable to the affected actors.

I then used this model to analyze three sets of innovations. I began with the centralization of meat cutting. I then went on to the computerization of the checkstands. And finally, I analyzed the decentralization of decision making to the shop floor. Each of these cases illustrates some important lessons for our understanding of the innovation process.

Perhaps the most interesting of these innovations, for organizational sociology and business managers, is the decentralization that gave more autonomy to shop-floor employees. Increasing worker participation is an important theme in the current business literature. This study leads to some insights into the decentralization process, and, in particular, into some of the areas in which problems are likely to occur. These areas include the problems of worker control, worker training, and worker status. SuperStores recognized that in order to compete in many heterogeneous markets against competitors who were well adapted to local conditions, they had to shorten information flows in the organization. They did this by creating the entrepreneurial store—a semiautonomous unit that combined the economies of scale of a large firm (for example, in warehousing, advertising, and purchasing) with the flexibility of an independent store. Because of the large store size, flexibility and autonomy were extended to the department heads and store clerks as well. This decentralization gave SuperStores the ability to compete in numerous geographic and product markets. Flexibility was particularly important in the new specialty shops that produced for the table food market, a much more idiosyncratic market than the market for groceries.

Chapter 5 shows how these changes affected the workers, increasing their bundle of tasks to include more ordering, production, and customer-service tasks. However, such changes reorganized the relations in production. In particular, they changed the relations between workers and managers in ways that increased the threat of opportunism. By making the individual departments into profit centers and making the department head responsible for her group's performance, SuperStores could reduce the threat of opportunism by the newly autonomous workers.

Overall, the results from Chapter 5 suggest the following lessons for a successful decentralization. First, firms should give the unit that is at the source of uncertainty the autonomy to make decisions. This gives the firm flexibility in the face of uncertainty. Second, firms should give the workers enough training to enable them to act responsibly and to make the appropriate decisions in the face of uncertainty. Third, firms should make the workers responsible for their decisions. This will have two effects. It will reduce opportunism, and it will increase workers' pride in their work and their desire to make it successful. By giving workers a result to point to ("Mine was the third-best deli in the division in terms of sales growth"), this decentralization of profit accounting gives the workers the feedback needed to induce participation.

A strong store-based, or company-based, culture can also be an important contributor to a successful decentralization. Deal and Kennedy (1982), for example, discuss the importance of strong culture in successful companies. Such cultures give workers a set of guidelines for behavior that allows them to act in ways that will promote company goals, even in circumstances in which specific rules do not apply. A strong culture would therefore be particularly important in decentralized firms, where workers have a lot of autonomy. By socializing them into the corporate culture, firms can be more certain that workers will use their autonomy in ways that are consistent with the company's goals.

However, worker goals and firm goals do not always coincide. Hodson (1991) for example, develops a model of behavior in the workplace that contains two dimensions—one reflecting the application of effort to further firm goals, the other reflecting effort to advance the individual's goals. Hodson claims that, while not orthogonal, the two dimensions do diverge. The problem for the firm is to ensure that workers advance the goals of the firm. This effort does not necessarily result in suppressing individual goals. For example, by encouraging workers to focus on successfully accomplishing tasks that they have set (in negotiation with their supervisor), firms can further both the individual goal of self-actualization and the firm goal of increased productivity.

The experiences of SuperStores provide additional lessons for other firms trying to decentralize. Programs that give workers responsibility without autonomy (as is the case in many quality circles) can lead to workers withdrawing their participation. Programs that give workers autonomy without responsibility (tenured faculty, for example) can lead to opportunistic behavior. Programs that do not include enough training (including training in decision making) will not produce the results that a well-trained work force can produce. Training provides workers with an extensive set of decision rules, making them better able to respond appropriately to a variety of environmental cues (Simon 1976, Stinchcombe 1990). In addition, investment in training is a sign that the firm is serious about its commitment to participation, further increasing the workers' desires to participate. Firms that want to decentralize should try to find ways to give workers real decision-making authority (and not simply making them management staff, who advise but are not allowed to make independent decisions [cf. Simmons and Mares 1983, ch. 6]). They should also find ways of measuring performance at the local level and then giving workers feedback on the effects of their decisions on their performance. Gain-sharing plans are one type of feedback that ties worker rewards directly to performance. Freund and Epstein (1984) argue for aggregating performance measures to the plant or company level as a way of maximizing the fit between individual and organizational goals. However, decentralized systems that measure results at the level over which individual workers have the most control—the individual or work group level—may be more effective in inducing workers to contribute toward furthering company goals.

These worker-participation innovations may eliminate the need for some levels of management. Smith (1990) notes that middle-management resistance is one of the major problems with implementing flexible structures. These innovations reorganize the relations in the firm in ways that attack the core tasks of middle management, such as making operations decisions at the shop-floor level. One way to reduce resistance would be to upgrade these managers by giving them the autonomy and training to do more strategic planning and other high-status tasks.

The decentralization at SuperStores also highlighted the problem of worker status in the new organization. While workers had an increased bundle of tasks, these tasks were not highly valued, particularly the customer-service skills. Because of the cultural context (service skills are female and are considered part of the general socialization process of women), these workers were not able to translate their increased competence into increased status. In the case of SuperStores, the result was that its decentralization did not increase labor costs as much as they might if the newly required skills were more highly valued. While SuperStores recognized the importance of customer-service competence and invested in training programs to increase that competence, management was able to take advantage of the cultural context to limit the cost of using that competence. This example underscores the importance of cultural factors in determining worker status and of incorporating these factors into an understanding of innovation in organizations. Thomas (1985) has one of the best analyses of the interrelations between firms, the state, technology and the organization of work, and the gender and citizenship statuses of workers. He finds that the development of technology in lettuce harvesting was strongly influenced by immigration policy, lobbying by agriculture firms, the civil rights movements, union strength, and gender stratification. When changing immigration policy and greater union strength substantially increased the cost of skilled Mexicans to handpick the lettuce, firms adopted a capital-intensive, machine-driven process, staffed mainly by low-paid female citizens. My findings echo his conclusion that, in order to understand technological innovation, we need to include this larger context of the relations in production.

One aspect of customer service that prevents it from becoming a recognized skill is that it seems difficult to teach, in part because it is considered common sense and therefore is not analyzed. Because of this difficulty, it is hard to develop a formal means of transmitting the competence to a new generation of workers. It is also difficult to develop a general culture of service workers, which could use its cultural solidarity as a basis for monopoly closure. While each enterprise usually develops a worker culture that does get transmitted, the specificity of this culture, which deals primarily with company-specific rules or situations, or how to get along with particular bosses and coworkers (see Kusterer 1978), makes it difficult to translate it into legitimized closure, such as apprenticeship requirements, licensing, and work rules. Thus, it seems that an important step toward a class consciousness among service workers is the routinization and legitimation of a training program in the control of the workers, one that would allow the development of a general service worker culture, or at least an occupationally specific culture. Now, workers have only informal training in the stores, with some cross-store interaction under management control.

Service workers need to advance their group-based goal of more equitable compensation. Just as strong corporate cultures create the solidarity and drive needed to advance the firm's goals cooperatively, a strong occupationally based culture can help advance the collective interests of the occupation. One of the factors that accounts for the inequitable compensation of service workers in the supermarkets is a societal bias against women's work (see Reskin and Roos 1990). The service workers have no strong occupational culture to counteract this bias. To put it in terms of the politicized context model, service workers in the supermarkets are not an interest group, and so have no collective political power. Rather, they have allied themselves with the rest of the workers, through the union. I do not have the data to ascertain whether the resulting contracts have advanced the cause of the male-dominated jobs at the cost of the female-dominated jobs or if the alliance with the male-dominated jobs has brought the service workers higher rewards than they would have received bargaining separately. My hypothesis is that bargaining separately would yield a fairer distribution of a smaller pie. Further research may shed more light on this issue.

The second innovation analyzed was a more fundamentally technological change: the introduction of computers into stores. The most visible aspect of this innovation was the bar-code scanners at the front end. This change was the result of extensive negotiations among food suppliers, retailers, and equipment manufacturers and required adding a new relationship to the web, the Universal Product Codes Committee, to maintain the integrity of the coding system so that no two products have the same code. The change also generated extensive resistance from consumers and workers, who formed an alliance so each could better defend its own interests. These groups, because they were large and organized, were able to modify the innovation in some markets (sometimes using government to enforce their position) so that scanners were introduced without removing item pricing. This modified innovation reduced consumer fears of price manipulation and limited the reduction in hours that clerks feared.

This chapter also notes the secondary effect after the introduction of the computer—decentralization of ordering. Because the computer automated many of the paperwork tasks involved in ordering, it became easier for workers to add this high-status task to their bundle. In this case, the computer automated the low-status but labor-intensive tasks of pricing items and entering the price into the register, while allowing workers to add the high-status task of ordering. This case shows the flexibility of computer technology with respect to worker skill. While managers could have used the same technology to further deskill the workers (cf. Zuboff 1988), SuperStores implemented this technology in such a way as to increase worker skill and to facilitate the decentralization that was occurring at the same time. This example also shows how innovations build on each other. Once bar coding of product became nearly universal, it made sense to automate the ordering procedure. This automation, combined with increased store size, facilitated the decentralization of ordering. If we concentrate on too small a subset of the tasks affected by technological change, we will fail to understand its effects on worker competence and autonomy. Technological change, by modifying the context, will often facilitate further changes in the new relations in production. We should include these secondary effects in our analyses of the effects of an innovation on a work setting.

The case of centralized meat cutting illustrates the complicated path of innovation. While the environmental conditions (in particular, uncertainty and declining munificence) pushed for a change in in-store meat processing, initial attempts with frozen meat failed. Frozen meat was resisted by consumers and by retailers, in large part because the product upset existing routines for transporting, storing, and processing meat into table food. This innovation demanded too much reorganization in the web of relations. Boxed beef, an alternative form of centralization, solved the problems of high in-store labor costs, high transportation costs, and ordering uncertainty, with minimal disruption of the web of relations. The major actors that were adversely affected were the meatcutters. As we predicted, they resisted this innovation but were largely unsuccessful, in part because the innovation undermined their source of power. This innovation had a largely deskilling effect on the cutters, although they still maintained their core tasks of retail cutting, and they began to add customer-service tasks to their bundle. The case of centralized cutting partially supports the deskilling thesis that technological change increasingly divides the work and replaces skilled workers with semiskilled or unskilled operatives (Braverman 1974). However, this case also introduces the caveat that, in addition to management's desire for control, worker resistance and market context are also important factors for understanding technological change (Walsh [1989] makes this argument in more detail).

In Chapter 1, I discussed the distinction between those theorists who emphasized technology as the driving force in the organization of work (e.g., Braverman 1974, Edwards 1979) and those who emphasized the environment (Lawrence and Lorsch 1967, Perrow 1967, Thompson 1967). The technologists tended to emphasize the firm's desire for control, which should result in a decline in worker skill. The environmentalists tended to emphasize the firm's desire for flexibility in the face of uncertainty, which should lead to an increase in worker skill. Overall, the results from our analysis of the supermarket case are most consistent with an environmental perspective. While technology is important, environmental constraints seem to be driving both the intentions of management and the effects of innovations on workers. In the face of a heterogeneous and changing environment, firms adopted innovations that reduced uncertainty, often by giving more control to the workers.

Innovation and the Politicized Context Model

Technological change is more than simply the advance of science or management's desires to wrest knowledge and control away from the workers. Innovations upset the established social relations within an organization and between the organization and other organizations in its network. Technological change is thus not just a scientific process or an economic process. Rather it is both a social process and a political one. It is a social process in that it requires the development of a system of supports and integration among units to implement a change in what is an integrated system. One cannot easily change one part of the system without accounting for its effects on the rest of the system. The successful innovation is the result of both economic factors, such as concentration and market growth or decline, and social factors, such as who will be responsible for which parts of the new division of labor. Technically and economically feasible inventions will fail without the development of some mechanism for coordinating the new sets of activities. Also, determining which of several alternative forms of an innovation becomes adopted is heavily influenced by the structure in which they are embedded. Stinchcombe (1990) notes that because there are so many things that can fail in the process of developing a social system that will support the innovation, introducing innovations is not routinized even in large organizations. Innovations that target troublesome parts of the relations in production with minimum disturbance of other parts of the system will be the most successful. Diversification, for example, will tend to take advantage of established routines. Mechanization will be used to take over the routine tasks in a bundle but will fit with the rest of the division of labor. More radical inventions tend not to be introduced, not because they will not perform as promised but because implementing them requires reorganizing such a large number of relationships. Thus, introducing frozen meat was a more radical innovation than introducing boxed beef, not because the technology was more advanced (it was not) but because it upset more of the relations in the web. The simpler innovation eventually won out because more of the actors in the web could incorporate the innovation without upsetting existing routines. This result also suggests that it is easier to innovate in isolated parts of the structure. This is why setting up test plants is a good way of introducing radical innovations. The isolation of these plants makes it less necessary that they mesh their innovations with existing routines.

The innovation process is also political, in that the different groups affected by the change have vested interests in the outcome and will be variously able to influence that outcome. The evidence also suggests that a group is more likely to attempt a political intervention into the reorganization when the economies of the innovation are clearly opposed to the interests of that group. So, for example, cutters tried to prevent the sale of boxed beef through work rules, and clerks fought price removal in the legislatures because in both cases their labor was made redundant by the innovation. However, in the case of frozen meat, the new process was not cheaper or clearly superior so the cutters did not need to fight it. This result is obviously preliminary, and we need more systematic analyses to partial out exactly when political interventions into the innovation process will occur.

Thus, organizations are open systems tied into a network of other actors (Scott 1987). Implementing technological innovations requires developing a set of social relations that will either not interfere with existing practice (as in process innovations with respect to consumers) or will provide a satisfactory distribution of costs and benefits (Stinchcombe 1990). All the groups in the social system are political actors and can influence the final form of the innovation to the extent that they can mobilize their resources in their interests (Pfeffer 1981).

These cases from retail food as well as other industries, such as agriculture (Friedland, Barton, and Thomas 1981) and machining (Noble 1984), illustrate the importance of including such political and social factors in any theory of technological change. Otherwise, we run the risk of imputing motives for change (such as a desire for increased control) to the limited set of actors on which we concentrate, when, in fact, they were responding to pressures outside the organization. I have shown that the deskilling thesis is at best partially applicable to this industry. While some of the changes (boxed beef) did deskill workers, other changes (decentralization) increased worker skill. Computerization decreased demand and increased the pace of work for some of the workers (checkers), eliminated certain tasks like pricing for the stockers (in some markets), and also facilitated including the high-status task of ordering into the stocker's bundle. This change is clearly not a simple degradation of the work.

These cases are particularly informative because they were from a competitive industry with reasonably large firms and declining profits. Economic arguments suggest that firms in the industry should adopt any cost-saving innovations that are available. Most of the innovations examined lowered costs.[1] Comparing the introduction of frozen meat, scanners, and boxed beef—of which one was not adopted, one was modified, and one was adopted—suggests that power has some influence. The success of an innovation depends on a combination of the coalitions that are formed and their political contingencies, as well as the economics of the innovation.

Also, different actors will dominate different innovations. Process innovations are likely to be dominated by the managers and the workers, and perhaps the suppliers (cf. boxed beef). Product innovations are likely to be dominated by consumer interests. Innovations that affect consumers and workers are likely to lead to state intervention (e.g., price marking legislation for scanners).

In addition, even where all of the parties agree that they want the innovation and all find it economically rational, they can still have the social problem of how to reorganize the social structure to accommodate the innovation. For example, while suppliers and retailers both favored the introduction of scanners, they still had problems developing a set of relations that would allow the change. It took a joint committee to develop a set of standards for the industries involved.

I have also shown that, while all innovations have the potential for generating political action, not all do. For example, as predicted in Figure 1.4, workers are much more likely to resist innovations that attack their core tasks (boxed beef) or that add low-status tasks than they are to resist changes that either add high-status tasks (ordering) or remove low-status tasks (meat clerks). In addition, the results suggest an extension to the simplified task status by task addition-removal model presented in Figure 1.4. The case of the meatcutters' response to the meat clerks and the case of the grocery clerks' response to scanners both suggest that workers are less likely to resist the removal of tasks (wrapping and customer service for cutters, manual checking for grocery clerks) during times of rising demand. While changes may reduce the relative demand for a given type of worker, the rising overall demand may make workers more likely to acquiesce to the change. Thus, we should expand the model in Figure 1.4 to include the effects of context factors (such as changing demand) on political actions.

I have focused on the addition or removal of tasks and have noted that various tasks have higher or lower status. However, the case of meatcutters' reaction to the removal of the sales transaction when they were first moved into the stores (see Chapter 3) suggests that even low-status tasks (the selling transaction) can have symbolic importance. In this case, the loss of this task resulted in a loss of autonomy for the cutters. It was this attack on their autonomy, rather than the loss of this task, that the cutters resisted. Again, this response suggests that the model should include some weighting not only for the status of the tasks but also for their symbolic significance.

Finally, in the politicized context model in Figure 1.3, there are important interactions between the market context and the political contingencies that influence the outcome of an innovation. For example, the case of boxed beef shows how an invention can eliminate much of the basis of power of one of the actors. Shaiken (1984, ch. 8) argues that we should implement legislation (a technology bill of rights) that recognizes the workers' (and the community's) position in the web of relations and guarantees that they receive proper protection from the costs and share in the benefits of innovation. In addition, being a member of a privileged firm, such as a monopoly or oligopoly, gives the actors certain powers that are tied to the power of the organization. For example, firms in regulated industries often have well-paid union workers. After deregulation, many of these unions were forced to make concessions because the market positions of their respective firms were such that the firms could no longer pass the costs of high wages on to the consumer (Benjamin 1986). Thus (using Figure 1.3) context also influences contingencies. Innovations also influence both context and contingencies. We might try to develop models that include these feedback elements and collect data that will allow us to compare the more complicated models with the simplified model presented here.

Further Research

This study sets the groundwork for several follow-up studies. We can expand the generalizability of the model by collecting more wide-ranging data, either quantitative or qualitative, across more industries, or within this industry across more innovations. For example, subsequent studies might attempt to quantify the power components of the decision to innovate to see if the econometric models of innovation can be expanded to include the influence of strategic coalitions in the process. Similarly, case studies of innovations in other industries could trace the historical factors that influenced the adoption of one innovation over another. Noble's (1984) analysis of the adoption of numerically controlled machine tools in the United States is a good example of such a study. Also, this study focuses on externally generated innovations. While I suspect that similar processes apply to internally generated innovations, with the actors then being departments and not separate organizations (Bacharach and Lawler 1980, Pfeffer 1981, Wilson 1966), proving such a supposition would require empirical evidence.

One issue that needs further clarification is the nature of the fit process that led to the development of innovations such as the decentralized structure. I have suggested that the process was the result of rational responses by management to changing environmental contingencies, which resulted in part because of a deliberate diversification strategy. However, an alternative explanation for the change in structure was that SuperStores adopted these forms as a result of mimetic or other institutional processes (DiMaggio and Powell 1983, Eisenhardt 1988, Meyer and Rowan 1977, Tolbert 1985). As Drazin and Van de Ven (1985) and Gresov (1989) have noted, one of the weaknesses of many contingency theories is a poorly operationalized concept of fit. As others have noted, structural change in an industry can follow a two-stage process, with innovators responding to environmental factors and later firms following institutional factors (Fligstein 1985). In this study I have not attempted to test directly for differences between environmental and institutional factors that led to these changes. I have shown that, at various levels in the organization, SuperStores had associated the organizational change with changes in their contingencies. Further study may be able to uncover the extent to which this form of decentralization diffused through the supermarket industry and how much of this diffusion was the result of environmental factors and how much was institutional.

Learning from the Supermarket Case

There are several ways in which the supermarket industry is different from other industries. First, it is a very competitive, low-margin, high-volume industry. To the extent that monopoly power allows firms to buffer themselves from some of the forces I have postulated, they may find the innovation process less complicated. Also, much of the product is perishable and the markets are local, so workers and consumers in this industry have more power than might be the case in many industries. For example, even though some would argue that the work is relatively low skill, the industry is fairly heavily unionized (about 37% in the mid-1980s, compared to

19% for all industries and 27% for all manufacturing industries [Adams 1985]).[2] Newspapers are another industry with similar market conditions and that, until fairly recently, had a history of strong unions. This suggests that workers in retail food and similar industries are more successful at mobilizing than may be the case in other industries.

The industry is also highly visible and has been the subject of several attempts by the state to regulate operations. For example, the industry was one of the last to be released from the wage and price controls of the early 1970s (along with construction and health care) (PG January 1975). In industries that are not so visible to the public, changes might not be so political.

Finally, the industry is a retail industry. While it engages in production and service, its prime function is moving goods from suppliers to customers. Perhaps the innovation process might be different if the customer were another organization. However, the cases of both boxed beef and scanners show that innovation involves similar processes if the consumer of the innovation, which was the retailer in both cases, is an organization and not the public.

Thus, there are several ways in which the supermarket industry is different from other industries, so we should be cautious in generalizing these findings to other industries and occupations that are very different from this case. Yet, despite these differences, there are enough similarities between this case and other cases previously studied to suggest that what we learn here may be applicable to a variety of circumstances.

This study should inform us not only of the retail food industry but also of work and organizations in general. I have argued that the retail food industry is economically, culturally, and politically central in the United States today. Because this is such an important industry in its own right, it is worthwhile to study it to see if the theories developed in other domains apply. For example, while the theory of decentralization is well developed, this industry gives us some interesting insights. First, while much of the literature on decentralization concerns the diffusion of management functions from the central office to the division or plant level, this study shows how the process can continue down to the level of the shop floor, with hourly employees being held responsible for profits in their subunits. Also, while

Piore and Sabel (1984) and others (e.g., Burris 1989, Perrow 1991) have pointed to the ability of skilled craftsmen and professionals to direct their own work and thereby make small firms (and certain types of large firms) responsive to market demand, I have shown that nominally low-skilled workers (grocery clerks) in large firms can also be used as part of a flexible strategy because of the shop-floor knowledge they possess.

I have also shown that this organizational change interacts with the cultural context so that the increase in worker skill did not lead to a concomitant increase in status. I suspect other industries also take advantage of the cultural context by using women, ethnic and racial minorities, or elderly workers as low-cost sources of "common-sense" skills. The use of Hispanic women in the clothing industry on the West Coast is but one example (Light and Bonacich 1988).

Many of the issues I have found in retail food are very similar to those found in most other industries. For example, the problem of local demand, which was a major force in the development of Super-Stores' decentralized structure, seems particularly relevant for multi-national firms, where local demand is quite variable. This study suggests that multinational firms would do well do develop a decentralized structure that relies on local expertise to handle operations and that uses statistical controls to maintain order. For example, the success of Gruppo GFT, the Italian clothing manufacturer, can be attributed in large part to its ability to customize clothing lines and marketing strategies for local markets (Howard 1991).

I also suspect that innovations in all industries are likely to introduce such problems as customer and worker resistance and coordination difficulties between firms and their suppliers. Managers would do well to anticipate the vast implications of disrupting the established social relations when introducing a new invention. For example, buffering the changes (using test plants) can reduce disruptions and thereby reduce resistance. Also, including affected actors (workers, consumers, community groups) into the decision-making process can reduce resistance by giving these groups a voice (Hirschman 1970), as well as by coopting potential sources of resistance (Selznick 1953). Similarly, when labor unions develop strategies for fighting undesirable innovations, they are more likely to be successful if they target aspects of the innovation that affect other actors with power, such as consumers. For example, public interest commercials that educate consumers about how an innovation affects them may help enlist consumer support in a fight against the change.

THUS, TECHNOLOGICAL AND organizational changes are complicated processes, because they have such far reaching implications. Only by attempting to capture this complexity in our theories can we fully understand the trajectory of technological and organizational innovations. This line of research has policy implications as well as theoretical interest. By understanding the process of innovation, in particular its social and political elements, we may be better able to develop policies that will encourage a more efficient process. For example, other industries might adopt organizations such as the Universal Product Code Committee to coordinate and oversee the implementation of innovations that requires multiorganization cooperation.

I have developed a model of innovation that describes the components of the process of technological or organizational change. This study provides the foundation for future research to help specify the parameters of that process.

NOTES

1. Introduction

1. In the example of finishing drywall, members of the two occupations actually struggled to get this task, which fell between the two occupations' established bundles. The final division of tasks was a compromise, with painters doing the work east of the Mississippi and carpenters doing it in the West (Stinchcombe 1990, ch. 2).

2. The following section is based on Harrington (1962), Brody (1964), and United Food and Commercial Workers (UFCW) archives.

3. The UFCW also includes the former Fur and Leather Workers, Packinghouse Workers, Boot and Shoe Workers, Barbers and Beauticians and the Insurance Workers Unions.

4. Sales in grocery stores account for almost 94% of total retail food sales (US BLS 1985). Supermarkets (currently defined as stores with annual sales of over $2 million) account for over 70% of grocery store sales.

5. *Progressive Grocer*, a monthly trade journal, has been published since 1922. It is targeted to grocery executives and store managers. In 1989, *Progressive Grocer's* circulation was approximately 90,000. There were approximately 150,000 grocery stores in 1989 (*PG* April 1990).

2. Environmental Changes during the Postwar Period

1. In real terms (adjusting for inflation) wages decreased at an average of 5% per year from 1966 to 1970; declined at a rate of 4% per year from 1971 to 1975; but increased at a rate of 7% per year from 1976 to 1980.

2. Even in 1990, women were the primary grocery shoppers in 70% of U.S. households (*PG* April 1991).

3. An alternative interpretation is that this demand for service may have been as strong in a previous generation but that firms were making sufficient profits and so were able to ignore it. Following this reasoning, one would argue that firms began to respond to this latent demand when slowing population growth increased competition and lowered profits. Thus, this shift toward service is consistent with a theory of management that assumes that firms are merely sufficing, and rather than innovating

when existing procedures become nonmaximum, only innovate when existing procedures start to become untenable (March and Simon 1958).

3. The Degradation of Work?: The Meatcutters

1. Shaiken (1984) notes similar reliability problems when firms attempted to develop workerless manufacturing systems. While managers may want to eliminate worker input, the inherent variability in the production process often makes complete automation less viable than a system that integrates machines and workers. However, such systems often use workers as flexible adjuncts to a rapid, machine-paced system, as illustrated rather vividly in the documentary film *Electronic Sweat-shop* (Bissonette 1985).

2. While there were several reports of store-based or chain-based frozen meat programs, these isolated experiments had only limited abilities to exploit the advantages of centralization. In the words of an owner of a store with a store-based frozen meat program: "Here's a big factor, though. If frozen meat retailing comes about it will, in my opinion, come largely through the meat packer or centralized level. These fellows will have a lot to say and do with the retailing of frozen meats of all grades" (*PG* November 1954: 62).

3. This higher price is somewhat misleading, since frozen cuts are boneless and were compared to bone-in cuts. However, the higher cost does discourage sales, even if the customer figures in the cost of the bone (*PG* December 1955).

4. For a more detailed analysis of the transportation advantages of standardized packaging, see Finlay (1988).

5. The newspaper typesetters suffered from a similar problem. The introduction of computerized typesetting eliminated much of the technical basis of the typesetters' power (Cockburn 1987, Roos 1990, Wallace and Kalleberg 1982). For example, when the typesetters went on strike against the *Chicago Tribune* in 1985 to protest the company's demands for concessions, their strike had little effect, because their skills were no longer part of the production process. The strike lasted for 40 months, with the workers finally settling for a buyout of their now nonexistent jobs (*Chicago Tribune* November 21, 1988, *Reader* November 11, 1988).

6. One result of the adoption of centralized meat processing as standard practice has been an increased concentration in the meat-packing industry. Table 3.2 shows the four firm concentration ratios for meat packing. During the postwar era, the concentration ratio continuously declined, from 41% in 1947 to a low of 19% in 1977. But, during the eighties, with the spread of boxed beef and the growth of IBP, concentration began to increase, and by 1987, it had risen to 32%.

4. Computerization in the Supermarkets

1. Shaiken also points out that, in case using obscure languages is not sufficient, some machines come with a locking cover for the control panel, to prevent "unauthorized use" (1984: 111).

2. Almost all systems developed still required the use of a checker. Currently some stores are experimenting with self-service checkout lanes (*Dow-Jones* Novem-

ber 13, 1989; *Chicago Sun-Times* July 19, 1991). In one such system, the customer would scan her own groceries and then take the receipt to the front desk, where she would pay the total. A bagger would still be available and would not only provide the service of bagging, but could also answer questions about how the checkstand worked, and could watch to make sure the customer scanned all of her items. Such systems are in the experimental stage, and it is too early to tell if this will become standard practice. However, given the high productivity of checkers with scanners and customer preferences for convenience, I suspect that under current conditions such systems will not become standard practice. Clerks would resist the loss of hours, customers would resist the inconvenience of multiple lines, and retailers would have only a mild interest in the slight cost savings. However, a change in context or a modification of the self-service checkout system (such as automating the payment transaction using a credit card or ATM card) could shift the balance in favor of self-service checkouts.

3. The need to change prices and the need to match prices to local markets and strategies limited the centralization alternative (having food manufacturers print prices on the items).

4. The remaining employees were divided among the meat and specialty departments or were produce clerks and baggers (who do not price but who are in the clerk's union).

5. The industry claimed that shelf tags were superior to item pricing for price comparisons, since shelf tags often included unit pricing (*PG* December 1975). However, in my observations, shelf tags were poorly maintained, and it was difficult for consumers to find the tags to compare various items.

6. Most checkers are female (Table 1.4).

7. For example, in 1990, almost 70% of consumers shopped in two or more stores per week (*PG* April 1991).

8. When ordering was the job of the store manager or head grocery, it was primarily a male job. When the task was decentralized, more women began to do the ordering (though still a minority). I will use the generic he for the rest of this section.

9. There are some fixed costs such as getting out the book and phoning the order (assuming the items come from the same vendor), so there are some economies.

5. Diversification and Its Effects on the Shop Floor

1. The department head is an hourly employee in charge of ordering, scheduling, and supervising for the whole department. She also engages in direct production. She is a member of the clerks' union, but her wages are determined by store volume, rather than seniority. The department head is a cross between a foreman and a gang boss—both a manager and a worker.

2. While this quote from a meatcutter has an obvious potential bias, his remarks are consistent with comments about the meat department by the other workers and managers I interviewed.

3. For example, they could change the product mix or buy from alternative sources, but they could not make major capital improvements.

4. This figure is an estimate based on data from *Progressive Grocer* (October 1982); McLaughlin, German, and Uetz (1986); and interviews with store managers.

5. A typical deli might have about 30 different salads and side dishes.

6. In 1990, 14% of stores had a sit-down restaurant (*PG* April 1991).

7. Workers in the meat department have traditionally had a great deal of autonomy (see Chapter 3).

8. Long lines at the checkout was the most common complaint.

9. This was when minimum wage was $3.35 per hour.

10. SuperStores, like many firms in the industry, had a two-tiered contract for many positions (Martin 1990, Walsh 1988).

11. Trist et al. (1963) describe a decentralized work structure consisting of groups of interdependent workers that were rewarded according to group performance, making the group responsible for internal governance.

12. On the other hand, ownership itself is not sufficient. Whyte and Blasi (1984) compare a variety of worker-ownership models, including Mondragon cooperatives, Isreali kibbutzim, union buyouts in the United States, and plywood cooperatives in the northwestern states. They argue that unless ownership is accompanied by participation, there is a strong tendency to revert to nonownership forms.

13. The store manager is usually consulted before someone is fired.

6. Conclusion

1. The data on frozen beef are weaker than those for the other innovations, but frozen beef had the same labor-saving advantages as boxed beef so it is likely that it produced at least some cost savings.

2. Comparable numbers for the mid-1970s are about 40% in retail food, 25% for all industries, and 45% for all manufacturing industries (Kochan 1980). These numbers illustrate the overall decline in unionization during this period.

BIBLIOGRAPHY

Abbott, Andrew. 1989. "The New Occupational Structure." *Work and Occupations* 16:273–291.

Abernathy, W. J. 1978. *The Productivity Dilemma: Roadblocks to Innovation in the Automobile Industry*. Baltimore: Johns Hopkins University Press.

Adams, Larry T. 1985. "Changing Employment Patterns of Organized Workers." *Monthly Labor Review* 108:25–31.

Attewell, P. "The Deskilling Controversy." *Work and Occupations* 14:323–346.

Bacharach, Samuel B., and Edward J. Lawler. 1980. *Power and Politics in Organizations*. San Francisco: Jossey-Bass.

Baldwin, W. L., and J. T. Scott. 1987. *Market Structure and Technological Change*. New York: Harwood.

Becker, Howard S. 1980. *Role and Career Problems of the Chicago Public School Teacher*. New York: Arno Press.

———. 1985. "Software for Sociologists: Finding Facts and Mastering Data." *Contemporary Sociology* 14:450–451.

Becker, Howard S., Andrew C. Gordon, and Robert K. LeBailly. 1984. "Field Work with the Computer: Criteria for Assessing Systems." *Qualitative Sociology* 7:16–33.

Beechey, V. 1982. "The Sexual Division of Labour and the Labour Process." In *The Degradation of Work*, edited by S. Wood, pp. 54–73. London: Hutchinson.

Benjamin, Daniel K. 1986. "Combinations of Workmen: Trade Unions in the American Economy." In *Unions in Transition*, edited by Semour M. Lipset, pp. 201–220. San Francisco: ICS.

Benton, L., T. R. Bailey, T. Noyelle, and T. M. Starback, Jr. 1991. *Employee Training and U.S. Competitiveness*. Boulder, CO: Westview.

Bielby, William T. 1991. "Sex Segregations, Gender Stereotypes and the Impact of Lucky Stores' Personnel Policies on Women Employees' Opportunities for Advancement." Unpublished paper. University of California, Santa Barbara.

Bissonette, Sophie (director). 1985. *The Electronic Sweatshop*. Distributed by California Newsreel.

Braverman, Harry. 1974. *Labor and Monopoly Capital*. New York: Monthly Review Press.

Brody, David. 1964. *The Butcher Workmen*. Cambridge: Harvard University Press.

Buchanan, D., and Boddy, D. 1983. *Organizations in the Computer Age: Technological Imperatives and Strategic Choice*. Aldershot, Eng.: Gower.

Bucklin, Louis P. 1980. "Technological Change and Store Operations: The Supermarket Case." *Journal of Retailing* 56:3–15.

Buffalo News. July 24, 1989. "Does Everything Need a Price Tag? Activists, Big Grocers Disagree." B:1.

Burkhardt, Marlene E., and Daniel J. Brass. 1990. "Changing Patterns or Patterns of Change: The Effects of a Change in Technology on Social Network Structure and Power." *Administrative Science Quarterly* 35:104–127.

Burns, Tom, and G. M. Stalker. 1961. *The Management of Innovation*. Chicago: Quadrangle.

Burris, Beverly H. 1989. "Technocratic Organization and Control." *Organization Studies* 10:1–22.

Chandler, Alfred D. 1962. *Strategy and Structure*. Cambridge: MIT Press.

Chicago Sun-Times. July 19, 1991. "Grocery Shoppers to Try Do-It-Yourself Checkout." 1:1.

Chicago Tribune. November 21, 1988. "Tribune Strike Nears End." 2:4.

Child, John. 1972. "Organizational Structure, Environment, and Performance: The Role of Strategic Choice." *Sociology* 6:1–22.

———. 1977. *Organization*. London: Harper and Row.

———. 1985. "Managerial Strategies, New Technology, and the Labour Process." In *Job Redesign: Critical Perspectives on the Labour Process*, edited by David Knights, Hugh Willmott, and David Collinson, pp. 107–141. Aldershot, Eng: Gower.

Clark, Kim B. W., Bruce Chew, and Takahiro Fujimoto. 1987. "Product Development in the World Auto Industry." *Brookings Papers on Economic Activity* 3:729–771.

Cockburn, Cynthia. 1987. "Gender, Technology, and Work: Contradictions and Skill in Printing," Paper presented at the Annual Meeting of the Society for the Study of Social Problems, Chicago.

Cohen, Wesley M., and Richard C. Levin. 1990. "Empirical Studies of Innovation and Market Structure." In *Handbook of Industrial Organization*, vol. 2, edited by R. Schmalenses and R. Willig, pp. 1059–1107. New York: North Holland Publishers.

Cole, Robert E. 1985. "The Macropolitics of Organizational Change: A Comparative Analysis of the Spread of Small-Group Activities." *Administrative Science Quarterly* 30:560–585.

Cornell University. Various years. *Operating Results of Food Chains*.

Cotterill, Ronald W. 1986. "Market Power in the Retail Food Industry." *Review of Economics and Statistics* 68:379–386.

Cotton, J. L., D. A. Vollrath, K. L Froggatt, M. L. Lengnick-Hall, and K. R. Jennings. 1988. "Employee Participation." *Academy of Management Review* 13:8–23.

Coyle, J. S. 1978. "Scanning Lights Up a Dark World for Grocers." *Fortune*, March 27, 1978, pp. 76–80.

Cyert, Richard M., and James G. March. 1963. *A Behavioral Theory of the Firm*. Englewood Cliffs, NJ: Prentice-Hall.

Daniel, W. W. 1987. *Workplace Industrial Relations and Technical Change*. Longmead, Eng: Frances Printer.

Daniels, A. K. 1988. *Invisible Careers*. Chicago: University of Chicago Press.

Deal, Terence E., and Allan A. Kennedy. 1982. *Corporate Cultures*. Reading, MA: Addison-Wesley.

DeVault, M. 1984. *Women and Food: Housework and the Production of Family Life*. Ph.D. dissertation. Evanston, IL: Northwestern University.

DiMaggio, Paul J., and Walter W. Powell. 1983. "The Iron Cage Revisited." *American Sociological Review* 48:147–160.

Dow-Jones News Service. November 11, 1989. "Supermarkets Test Self-Service System at Checkout Counter."

Downs, George W, Jr., and Lawrence B. Mohr. 1976. "Conceptual Issues in the Study of Innovation." *Administrative Science Quarterly* 21:700–714.

Drazin, Robert, and Andrew H. Van de Ven. 1985. "Alternative Forms of Fit in Contingency Theory." *Administrative Science Quarterly* 30:514–39.

Economist. April 27, 1991. *A Survey of International Finance*.

Edwards, Richard. 1979. *Contested Terrain*. New York: Basic Books.

Eisenhardt, Kathleen M. 1988. "Agency- and Institutional-Theory Explanations: The Case of Retail Sales Compensation." *Academy of Management Journal* 31:488–511.

Emerson, Richard M. 1962. "Power-Dependence Relations." *American Sociological Review* 27:31–41.

Ettlie, John E. 1983. "Organizational Policy and Innovation among Suppliers to the Food Processing Sector." *Academy of Management Journal* 26:27–44.

Finlay, William D. 1988. *Work on the Waterfront*. Philadelphia: Temple.

Fleet, Rex M. 1985. "Banking in Supermarkets." *The Magazine of Bank Administration* 61:38–40.

Fligstein, Neil. 1985. "The Spread of the Multidivisional Form among Large Firms, 1919–1979." *American Sociological Review* 50:377–391.

Fligstein, Neil, and Kenneth Dauber. 1989. "Structural Change in Corporate Organizations." *Annual Review of Sociology* 15: 73–96.

Forbes. October 25, 1982. "Flower Power." Pp. 75–76.

Freeman, R. B., and J. L. Medoff. 1984. *What Do Unions Do?* New York: Basic Books.

Freidman, A. 1977. *Industry and Labour*. London: Macmillan.

Freidson, E. 1975. *Doctoring Together: A Study of Professional Social Control*. New York: Elsevier.

Friedland, William H., Amy E. Barton, and Robert J. Thomas. 1981. *Manufacturing Green Gold*. New York: Cambridge University Press.

Freund, William C., and Eugene Epstein. 1984. *People and Productivity: The New York Stock Exchange Guide to Financial Incentives and the Quality of Work Life*. Homewood, IL: Dow Jones-Irwin.

Galbraith, Jay. 1973. *Designing Complex Organizations*. Reading, MA: Addison-Wesley.

Glazer, N. Y. 1984. "Servants to Capital: Unpaid Domestic Labor and Paid Work." *Review of Radical Political Economics* 16:61–87.

Glenn, E. N., and R. L. Feldberg. 1982. "Degraded and Deskilled: The Proletarianization of Clerical Work." In *Women and Work*, edited by Rachel Kahn-Hunt, Arlene Kaplan Daniels, and Richard Colvard, pp. 202–217. New York: Oxford.

Gresov, Christopher. 1989. "Exploring Fit and Misfit with Multiple Contingencies." *Administrative Science Quarterly* 34:431–453.

Gyllenhammar, P. G. 1977. *People at Work*. Reading, MA: Addison-Wesley.

Halle, David. 1984. *America's Working Man.* Chicago: University of Chicago Press.

Harrington, Michael. 1962. *The Retail Clerks.* New York: John Wiley and Sons.

Heskett, James L. 1986. *Managing in the Service Economy.* Boston: Harvard Business School.

Hickson, D. J., C. R. Hinings, C. A. Lee, R. E. Schneck, and J. M. Pennings. 1971. "A Strategic Contingencies Theory of Intraorganizational Power." *Administrative Science Quarterly* 16:216–229.

Hirschman, Albert O. 1970. *Exit, Voice, and Loyalty.* Cambridge: Harvard University Press.

Hobsbawm, E. J. 1964. *Labouring Men.* London: Weidenfeld and Nicolson.

Hochschild, A. R. 1983. *The Managed Heart.* Berkeley: University of California Press.

Hodson, Randy. 1991. "Workplace Behaviors: Good Soldiers, Smooth Operators and Saboteurs." *Work and Occupations* 18: 271–290.

Homans, George C. 1974. *Social Behavior: Its Elementary Forms.* Revised edition. New York: Harcourt Brace Jovanovich.

Howard, Robert. 1991. "The Designer Organization." *Harvard Business Review* 6 (5) (September–October 1991):28–44.

Hughes, Everett C. 1984. *The Sociological Eye.* New Brunswick, NJ: Transaction Books.

Jolly, D. Leeann, James W. Grimm, and Paul R. Wozniak. 1990. "Patterns of Sex Desegregation in Managerial and Professional Specialty Fields, 1950–1980." *Work and Occupations* 17:30–54.

Jones, Bryn. 1982. "Destruction or Redistribution of Engineering Skills?: The Case of Numerical Control." In *The Degradation of Work?: Skill, Deskilling and the Labour Process*, edited by Stephen Wood, pp. 179–200. London: Hutchinson.

Juravich, T. 1985. *Chaos on the Shop Floor.* Philadelphia: Temple University Press.

Kanter, R. M. 1983. *The Change Masters.* New York: Simon and Schuster.

Katz, Donald R. 1987. *The Big Store.* New York: Penguin.

Kirstein, George G. 1950. *Stores and Unions.* New York: Fairchild.

Kochan, Thomas A. 1980. *Collective Bargaining and Industrial Relations.* Homewood, IL: Richard D. Irwin.

Kraft, P. 1979. "The Industrialization of Computer Programming." In *Case Studies in the Labor Process*, edited by A. Zimbalist, pp. 1–17. New York: Monthly Review Press.

Kusterer, Ken C. 1978. *Know-How on the Job: The Important Working Knowledge of "Unskilled" Workers.* Boulder, CO: Westview Press.

Lamm, R. McFall. 1981. "Prices and Concentration in the Food Retailing Industry." *Journal of Industrial Economics* 30 (September):67–78.

Lawrence, Paul. 1958. *The Changing of Organizational Behavior Patterns: A Case Study of Decentralization.* Boston: Harvard University Press.

Lawrence, Paul R., and Jay W. Lorsch. 1967. *Organization and Environment.* Cambridge: Harvard University Press.

Laycock, G. 1983. *The Kroger Story: A Century of Innovation.* Cincinnati: Kroger Co.

Leidner, Robin. 1988. *Working on People: The Routinization of Interactive Service Work.* Ph.D. dissertation. Evanston, IL: Northwestern University.

Levin, Sharon G., Stanford L. Levin, and John B. Meisel. 1985. "Intermarket Differences in the Early Diffusion of an Innovation." *Southern Economic Journal* 51:672–680.

————. 1987. "A Dynamic Analysis of the Adoption of a New Technology: The Case of Optical Scanners." *Review of Economics and Statistics* 69:12–17.

Light, Ivan H., and Edna Bonacich. 1988. *Immigrant Entrepreneurs.* Berkeley: University of California Press.

McDonald, W.O., project director. 1982. "Project E: Is This the Team of the 80's?" Unpublished report. Cincinnati: Kroger Co.

McLaughlin, E. W., G. A. German, and M. P. Uetz. 1986. *The Economics of the Supermarket Delicatessen.* Agricultural Economics Research Report, 86–23. Ithaca, NY: Cornell University.

Maltz, M., A. Gordon, and W. Freidman, with M. Buslik, R. LeBailley, P. Schnorr, D. Thomson, and J. P. Walsh. 1991. *Mapping Crime in Its Community Setting.* New York: Springer Verlag.

March, James G., and Herbert A. Simon. 1958. *Organizations.* New York: John Wiley and Sons.

Marion, B. W. 1979. *The Food Retailing Industry: Market Structure, Profits, and Prices.* New York: Praeger Publishers.

Marshall, H. L. 1970. *The Educational Experience of Meat Cutting Apprentices.* Ph.D. Dissertation, Department of Sociology, Northwestern University.

Martin, James. 1990. *Two-Tier Compensation Structures: Their Impact on Unions, Employers and Employees.* Kalamazoo, MI: W. E. Upjohn Institute for Employment Research.

Marx, Karl. 1967. *Capital.* New York: Vintage Books.

Meara, Hannah. 1974. "Honor in Dirty Work: The Case of American Meat Cutters and Turkish Butchers." *Work and Occupations* 1:259–283.

Mendelson, Anne. 1991. "Nutribabble." *The Nation,* June 17, 1991, pp. 825–827.

Meyer, John W., and Brian Rowan.1977. "Institutionalized Organizations." *American Journal of Sociology* 83:340–363.

Meyer, Marshall W., and Lynne G. Zucker. 1989. *Permanently Failing Organizations.* Newbury Park, CA: Sage.

Montgomery, David. 1979. *Workers' Control in America.* Cambridge, Eng.: Cambridge University Press.

More, C. 1980. *Skill and the English Working Class, 1870–1914.* New York: St. Martin's.

Mottaz, C. J. 1985. "The Relative Importance of Intrinsic and Extrinsic Rewards as Determinants of Work Satisfaction." *Sociological Quarterly* 26: 365–85.

New York Times. September 14, 1986. "What's New at the Supermarket."

————. November 8, 1989. "Supermarkets as Theater, Service as Star." C1.

Newsweek. November 10, 1986. "Filling a Tooth at the Grocery: Off to the Hypermarket." P. 59.

————. June 27, 1988. "Super-Duper Supermarkets." Pp. 40–41.

Noble, D.F. 1979. "Social Choice in Machine Tool Design: The Case of Automatically Controlled Machine Tools." In *Case Studies in the Labor Process,* edited by A. Zimbalist, pp. 18–50. New York: Monthly Review Press.

————. 1984. *Forces of Production.* New York: Knopf.

Ouchi, W. G. 1981. *Theory Z.* Reading, MA: Addison-Wesley.

Penn, R. 1892. "Skilled Manual Labour in the Labour Process, 1856–1964." In *The Degradation of Work?,* edited by S. Wood, pp. 90–121. London: Hutchinson.

Perrow, Charles. 1967. "A Framework for Comparative Organizational Analysis." *American Sociological Review* 32:194–208.

———. 1991. "Small Firm Networks." Keynote Speech. IAREP/SASE Conference, Stockholm.

Peters, Thomas J., and Robert H. Waterman. 1982. *In Search of Excellence.* New York: Harper and Row.

Pettigrew, Andrew M. 1972. "Information Control as a Power Resource." *Sociology* 6:187–204.

Pfeffer, Jeffrey. 1981. *Power in Organizations.* Cambridge, MA: Ballinger.

Pfeffer, Jeffrey, and Gerald Salancik. 1978. *External Control of Organizations.* New York: Harper and Row.

Pfeffer, Jeffrey, and Jerry Ross. 1990. "Gender-Based Wage Differences: The Effects of Organizational Context." *Work and Occupations* 17:55–78.

Pinchot, G. 1985. *Intrapreneuring.* New York: Harper and Row.

Piore, M. J., and C. F. Sabel.1984. *The Second Industrial Divide: Possibilities for Prosperity.* New York: Basic Books.

Porter, Glenn, and Harold C. Livesay. 1971. *Merchants and Manufacturers.* Baltimore: Johns Hopkins University Press.

Progressive Grocer. July 1951. "Take a Trip through One of New England's Finest New Markets!" Pp. 47–51. (In text, references to *Progressive Grocer* are cited as *PG* with date.)

———. November 1954. "Is This the Meat Department of the Future?" Pp. 57–94.

———. December 1955. "Merchandising Experience with Frozen Meats." Pp. 70–71.

———. February 1956. "Fresh-Frozen, Wax-Coated Meats Are Huge Success in Ohio Tests." Pp. 68–84.

———. July 1957. "Quantity Sales for Home Freezers Boost Meat Volume 33%." Pp. 123–142.

———. September 1957. "What's Ahead for Frozen Red Meats?" Pp. 186–196.

———. May 1958. "Customer's Meat Buying Habits Being Changed at Wrigley's." Pp. 165–166.

———. April 1968. "Trends in Meat Merchandising." Pp. 192–225.

———. March 1970. "Iowa Beef Packers Aims to Be Nation's Top Processor." Pp. 118–124.

———. July 1970. "Technology is Beefing up King of Meats." Pp. 102–106.

———. August 1971. "Wetterau Puts Profitability into Boxed beef." Pp. 74–80.

———. January 1972. "Universal Product Code Nears Reality." Pp. 90–94.

———. April 1972. "1971 Charts Key Trends for Meats." Pp.175–180.

———. January 1975. "Grocery Labor Is Aiming High This Year." Pp. 79–82.

———. March 1975. "UPC Scanning a Success at Marsh's." Pp. 59–63.

———. May 1975. "Update: Grocers May Head Off Item Pricing Law, But Cost Will Be Stiff." Pp. 40–41.

———. June 1975a. "Behind the Deli/Food Service Renaissance." Pp. 106–128.

———. June 1975b. "There's Still Fun and Profit in Meats." Pp. 59–62.

———. September 1975. "California Lawmakers Give Scanning a Break." P. 30.

———. December 1975. "Scanning Hits A Snag." Pp. 47–60.

———.February 1976a. "Many Roads to Success." Pp. 75–76.

———. February 1976b. "Serving up New Sales and Profits for Supers." Pp. 53–64.

————. April 1976. "Issues '76 / Labor." Pp. 55–59.

————. March 1978. "Small Independent Upstages Big Labor by Taking Issue to People, Politicians." P. 47.

————. July 1978. "Box Beef Keeps on Truckin'." P. 13.

————. February 1979. "How 340 Meat Items Sell." Pp. 35–45.

————. February 1980. "Produce Manager." Pp. 41–62.

————. March 1980. "Is the Meat Department Slipping?" Pp. 95–102.

————. April 1980. "Update: Labor Relations." Pp. 10–26.

————. Mid-May 1980. *Supermarkets: 50 Years of Progress.*

————. June 1981. "Service Lives." Pp. 31–56.

————. June 1982. "Cheese and Deli Shoppers." Pp. c1–c24.

————. October 1982. "Delibake Combination on a Roll." Pp. 107–116.

————. June 1983. "Delis: How They're Doing." P. c4.

————. December 1983 "Fresh Ideas For Produce." Pp. 79–92.

————. February 1984. "Deli/Bakery Digest: Spring 1984." P. f–6.

————. May 1984. "Service Departments: A Fresh Approach to Balancing the High Cost of Labor." Pp. 21–36.

————. September 1984. "Firing Line." P. 150.

————. October 1984. "Chains with Muscle: 10 Supermarket Giants."

————. November 1984. "Minyard Picks Up the Pace." Pp. 67–76.

————. December 1984. "Today Cincinnati, Tomorrow . . . ?" Pp. 21–22.

————. January 1985. "Firing Line." P. 94.

————. February 1985. "Pick'n'Save: Making It Famous in Milwaukee." Pp. 61–69.

————. March 1985. "A Call for Consolidation." Pp. 99–101.

————. June 1985a. "Hard Choice for Union Workers." Pp. 59–64.

————. June 1985b. "Meat Talk: 29 Winning Ways with Boxed Beef." Pp. 87–88.

————. January 1986a. "How to Coax Greater Productivity from the Front End." Pp. 89–94.

————. January 1986b. "What Will Turn Your Customers On—and Off." Pp. 31–41.

————. April 1987. *Annual Report on the Industry.*

————. May 1987. "College Grads Make the Retail Grade." Pp. 165–169.

————. April 1989. *Annual Report on the Industry.*

————. October 1989. "1989 Nielsen Review of Retail Grocery Store Trends." Pp. 41–57.

————. April 1990. *Annual Report on the Industry.*

————. April 1991. *Annual Report on the Industry.*

Raskin, A. H. 1986. "Labor: A Movement in Search of a Mission." In *Unions in Transition,* edited by Seymour M. Lipset, pp. 3–38. San Francisco: ICS.

Reader. November 11, 1988. "Strike Accord at the Tribune." 1:4.

Reskin, Barbara F., and Patricia A. Roos. 1990. *Job Queues, Gender Queues.* Philadelphia: Temple University Press.

Romeo, Anthony A. 1977. "The Rate of Imitation of a Capital-Embodied Process Innovation." *Economica* 44:63–69.

Roos, Patricia A. 1990. "Hot-Metal to Electronic Composition: Gender, Technology and Social Change." In *Job Queues, Gender Queues,* edited by Barbara F. Reskin and Patricia A. Roos, pp. 275–298. Philadelphia: Temple University Press.

Roethlisberger, F. J., and W. J. Dickson. 1939. *Management and the Worker.* Cambridge, MA: Harvard University Press.

Rosen, Corey. 1991. "Employee Ownership: Performance, Prospects and Promise." In *Understanding Employee Ownership,* edited by C. Rosen and K. M. Young, pp. 1–42. Ithaca, NY: ILR Press.

Rubenstein, A. H., and J. E. Ettlie. 1979. "Innovation among Suppliers to Automotive Manufacturers: An Exploratory Study of Barriers and Facilitators." *R&D Management* 9:65–76.

Sabel, Charles F. 1982. *Work and Politics.* Cambridge, Eng.: Cambridge University Press.

Schumpeter, J. A. 1942. *Capitalism, Socialism and Democracy.* New York: Harper and Row.

Scott, W. Richard. 1987. *Organizations: Rational, Natural and Open Systems.* 2d ed. Englewood Cliffs, NJ: Prentice-Hall.

Selznick, Philip. 1953. *TVA and the Grass Roots.* New York: Harper and Row.

Shaiken, Harley. 1984. *Work Transformed: Automation and Labor in the Computer Age.* New York: Holt, Rinehart, and Winston.

Simmons, John, and William Mares. 1983. *Working Together.* New York: Knopf.

Simon, Herbert A. 1976. *Administrative Behavior.* 3d edition. New York: Free Press.

Smith, Vicki. 1990. *Managing in the Corporate Interest.* Berkeley: University of California Press.

Sorge, Arndt, and Wolfgang Streeck. 1988. "Industrial Relations and Technical Change: The Case for an Extended Perspective." In *New Technology and Industrial Relations,* edited by Richard Hyman and Wolfgang Streeck, pp. 19–47. New York: Basil Blackwell.

Steiger, T., and B. F. Reskin. 1990. "Baking and Baking-Off: Deskilling and the Changing Sex Makeup of Bakers." In *Job Queues, Gender Queues,* edited by B. F. Reskin and P. A. Roos, pp. 257–274. Philadelphia: Temple University Press.

Stinchcombe, Arthur L. 1990. *Information and Organizations.* Berkeley: University of California Press.

Stone, K. 1974. "The Origins of Job Structures in the Steel Industry." *Review of Radical Political Economics* 6:61–97.

Strauss, A. 1985. "Work and the Division of Labor." *Sociological Quarterly* 26:1–20.

Taylor, Frederick W. 1911. *Principles of Scientific Management.* New York: Harper.

Thomas, Robert J. 1985. *Citizenship, Gender and Work.* Berkeley: University of California Press.

——. 1987. "Microchips and Macroharvests: Labor-Management Relations in Agriculture." In *Workers, Managers and Technological Change: Emerging Patterns of Labor Relations,* edited by Daniel B. Cornfield, pp. 27–45. New York: Plenum.

Thompson, James D. 1967. *Organizations in Action.* New York: McGraw-Hill.

Thompson, W. E. 1983. "Hanging Tongues: A Sociological Encounter with an Assembly Line" *Qualitative Sociology* 6:215–237.

Time. August 11, 1986. "A is for Apple? No, Atemoya." Pp. 61–62.

Tolbert, Pamela S. 1985. "Resource Dependence and Institutional Environments: Sources of Administrative Structure in Institutions of Higher Education." *Administrative Science Quarterly* 30:1–13.

Trist, E. L., G. W. Higgin, H. Murray, and A. B. Pollock. 1963. *Organizational Choice*. London: Tavistock.

Tushman, Michael L., and Philip Anderson. 1986. "Technological Discontinuities and Organizational Environments." *Administrative Science Quarterly* 31:439–465.

United Food and Commercial Workers Research Office. 1980. "The Retail Food Industry—How the Union Sees It". Paper presented to UFCW Retail Food Conference, Houston, TX. (In text, cited as UFCW with date.)

————. March–April, 1987. "What UFCW Members Think About Their Union." *UFCW Action* Pp. 10–12.

United States Bureau of the Census. 1971. *Statistical Abstract of the United States, 1971*. Washington, D.C.: Government Printing Office. (In text, cited as US Census with date.)

————. 1976. *Census of Retail Trade, 1972: v. 1 Summary and Subject Statistics*. Washington, D.C.: Government Printing Office.

————. 1977. *Census of Manufacturers: v. 1 Subject Statistics*. Washington, D.C.: Government Printing Office.

————. 1985. *Statistical Abstract of the United States: 1986, 106th edition*. Washington, D.C.: Government Printing Office.

————. 1987. *Census of Manufacturers: General Summary*. Washington, D.C.: Government Printing Office.

————. 1990. *Statistical Abstract of the United States: 1990*. Washington, D.C.: Government Printing Office.

————. 1991. *Statistical Abstract of the United States: 1991*. Washington, D.C.: Government Printing Office.

United States Bureau of Labor Statistics. 1972. *Occupational Employment Statistics, 1960–1970*. Washington, D.C.: U.S. Department of Labor, Bureau of Labor Statistics. (In text, cited as US BLS with date.)

————. 1973. *Union Wages and Hours: Grocery Stores, July 1, 1971*. Washington, D.C.: U.S. Department of Labor, Bureau of Labor Statistics.

————. 1975. *Union Wages and Hours: Grocery Stores, July 1, 1973*. Washington, D.C.: U.S. Department of Labor, Bureau of Labor Statistics.

————. 1976. *Union Wages and Hours: Grocery Stores, July 1, 1975*. Washington, D.C.: U.S. Department of Labor, Bureau of Labor Statistics.

————. 1978. *Union Wages and Hours: Grocery Stores, July 1, 1977*. Washington, D.C.: U.S. Department of Labor, Bureau of Labor Statistics.

————. 1981a. *Union Wages and Hours: Grocery Stores, September 4, 1979*. Washington, D.C.: U.S. Department of Labor, Bureau of Labor Statistics.

————. 1981b. *National Industry-Occupation Employment Matrix, 1970, 1978, and Projected 1990*. Washington, D.C.: U.S. Department of Labor, Bureau of Labor Statistics.

————. 1984. *Occupational Employment in Transportation, Communications, Utilities and Trade*. Washington, D.C.: U.S. Department of Labor, Bureau of Labor Statistics.

————. 1987. *The National Industry-Occupation Employment Matrix, 1984 and 1995 Projected*. Washington, D.C.: U.S. Department of Labor, Bureau of Labor Statistics.

————. 1990. *Occupational Employment in Selected Nonmanufacturing Industries*. Washington, D.C.: U.S. Department of Labor, Bureau of Labor Statistics.

Wallace, M., and A. L. Kalleberg. 1982. "Industrial Transformation and the Decline of Craft: The Decomposition of Skill in the Printing Industry, 1931–1978." *American Sociological Review* 47:307–324.

Walker, C. R., and R. H. Guest. 1952. *Man on the Assembly Line.* Cambridge, MA: Harvard University Press.

Walsh, John P. 1988. "How Well Do Unions Do It: Monopoly and Voice in a Two-Tiered Union." Paper presented at the Annual Meeting of the Midwest Sociological Society, Minneapolis.

———. 1989. "Technological Change and the Division of Labor: The Case of Retail Meatcutters." *Work and Occupations* 16:165–183.

Whalley, P. 1984. "Deskilling Engineers?" *Social Problems* 32:117–132.

Whyte, William F. 1961. *Men at Work.* Homewood, IL: Richard D. Irwin.

Whyte, William F., and Joseph R. Blasi. 1984. "Worker Ownership, Participation, and Control: Toward a Theoretical Model." In *Critical Studies in Organization & Bureaucracy,* edited by Frank Fischer and Carmen Sirianni, pp. 377–405. Philadelphia: Temple University Press.

Wilkinson, B. 1983. *The Shopfloor Politics of New Technology.* London: Heinemann.

Williamson, O. E. 1975. *Markets and Hierarchies, Analysis and Antitrust Implications.* New York: Free Press.

———. 1985. *The Economic Institutions of Capitalism.* New York: Free Press.

Wilson, James Q. 1966. "Innovation in Organization." In *Approaches to Organizational Design,* edited by James D. Thompson, pp. 193–218. Pittsburgh: University of Pittsburgh Press.

Wood, S., editor. 1982. *The Degradation of Work.* London: Hutchinson.

Wright, J. Patrick. 1979. *On a Clear Day You Can See General Motors.* Gross Pointe, MI: Wright Enterprises.

Zimbalist, A., editor. 1979. *Case Studies in the Labor Process.* New York: Monthly Review Press.

Zimmerman, M. M. 1955. *The Super-Market.* New York: McGraw-Hill.

Zuboff, S. 1988. *In the Age of the Smart Machine.* New York: Basic Books.

NAME INDEX

Abbott, Andrew, 38
Abernathy, W. J., 23
Adams, Larry T., 162
Aguilar, Carlos, xiii
Anderson, Philip, 62
Attewell, P., 20

Bacharach, Samuel B., 16, 26, 160
Bailey, T. R., 127, 134, 136
Baldwin, W. L., 24, 37
Barton, Amy E., 78, 158
Becker, Howard S., xiii, 27, 35
Beechey, V., 127, 140
Benjamin, Daniel K., 160
Benton, L., 127, 134, 136
Bielby, William T., xiii, 111
Bissonette, Sophie, 166
Blasi, Joseph R., 168
Boddy, D., 123
Bonacich, Edna, 163
Brass, Daniel J., 24, 71, 109
Braverman, Harry, 12, 13, 22, 30, 59, 70, 81, 88, 90, 155, 156
Bridges, William, xiii
Brody, David, 165
Buchanan, D., 123
Bucklin, Louis P., 32, 84, 94
Burkhardt, Marlene E., 24, 71, 109
Burns, Tom, 101
Burris, Beverly H., 163
Buslik, M., 26

Chandler, Alfred D., 9, 13, 30, 53, 109–110, 111, 115, 130
Chew, Bruce, 132
Child, John, 14, 16, 19, 95, 129, 130
Clark, Kim B. W., 132
Cockburn, Cynthia, 141, 145, 166
Cohen, Wesley, xiii, 23
Cole, Robert E., 15, 128
Cotterill, Ronald W., 57
Cotton, J. L., 131
Coyle, J. S., 95
Cyert, Richard M., 21, 69

Daniel, W. W., 26
Daniels, A. K., 141, 145
Dauber, Kenneth, 21, 36
Deal, Terence E., 151
DeVault, M., 29, 75, 115, 145
Dickson, W. J., 60
DiMaggio, Paul J., 21, 30, 161
Downs, George W. Jr., 20
Drazin, Robert, 161

Edwards, Richard, 13, 22, 59, 70, 129, 156
Eisenhardt, Kathleen M., 161
Emerson, Richard M., 24
Epstein, Eugene, 152
Ettlie, John E., 22, 23

Feldberg, R. L., 19
Feldman, Ackie, xiii

Finholt, Tom, xiii
Finlay, William D., xiii, 20, 166
Fleet, Rex M., 9
Fligstein, Neil, 9, 21, 23, 30, 36, 109, 111, 161
Freeman, R. B., 25, 70
Freidman, W., 26
Freidson, E., 125
Freund, William C., 152
Friedland, William H., 78, 158
Froggatt, K. L., 131
Fujimoto, Takahiro, 132

Galbraith, Jay, 13, 108
German, G. A., 109, 115, 118, 119, 141
Glazer, N. Y., 2, 23, 47, 62, 64, 92
Glenn, E. N., 19
Gordon, Andrew C., 26, 35, 169
Gresov, Christopher, 161
Grimm, James W., 145
Guest, R. H., 134
Gyllenhammar, P. G., 130

Halle, David, 20, 123
Harrington, Michael, 49, 98, 165
Heskett, James L., 15
Hickson, D. J., 16, 17, 24, 109
Higgin, G. W., 132, 168
Hinings, C. R., 16, 17, 24, 109
Hirschman, Albert O., 24, 25, 77, 93, 163
Hobsbawm, E. J., 24
Hochschild, A. R., 125, 144–145
Hodson, Randy, 151
Homans, George C., 66, 67
Howard, Robert, 163
Hughes, Everett C., 12, 27

Jablonski, Alfred, xiii
Jennings, K. R., 131
Jolly, D. Leeann, 145
Jones, Bryn, 22
Juravich, T., 20, 65

Kalleberg, A. L., 45, 91, 166
Kanter, R. M., 6, 117
Katz, Donald R., 55, 111, 132

Kennedy, Allan A., 151
Kirstein, George G., 96, 98
Kochan, Thomas A., 168
Kraft, P., 19, 145
Kusterer, Ken C., 20, 65, 153

Lamm, R. McFall, 93
Lammers, John, xiii
Lawler, Edward J., 16, 26, 160
Lawrence, Paul, 3, 13, 108, 110, 130, 131, 132, 156
Laycock, G., 60
LeBailley, Robert K., 26, 35, 169
Lee, C. A., 16, 17, 24, 109
Leidner, Robin, xiii, 125
Lengnick-Hall, M. L., 131
Levin, Richard C., 23
Levin, Sharon G., 16, 24, 32, 37, 95
Levin, Stanford L., 16, 24, 32, 37, 95
Light, Ivan H., 163
Livesay, Harold C., 26, 69, 72
Lorsch, Jay W., 13, 108, 132, 156

McDonald, W. O., 53
McLaughlin, E. W., 109, 115, 118, 119, 141
Maltz, M., 26
March, James G., 14, 16, 21, 45, 56, 69, 88, 166
Mares, William, 152
Marion, B. W., 57, 93, 100
Marshall, H. L., 27, 60, 61. See also Meara, Hanna
Martin, James, 168
Marx, Karl, 30, 90
Meara, Hannah, 69. See also Marshall, H. L.
Medoff, J. L., 25, 70
Meisel, John B., 16, 24, 32, 37, 95
Mendelson, Anne, 46
Meyer, John W., 21, 30, 161
Meyer, Marshall W., 21
Mohr, Lawrence B., 20
Montgomery, David, 113, 134
More, C., 134
Mottaz, C. J., 120
Murray, H., 132, 168

Noble, D. F., 19, 23, 105, 106, 158, 160
Norr, James, xiii
Noyelle, T., 127, 134, 136

Orum, Anthony, xiii
Ouchi, W. G., 6, 14, 15, 117

Penn, R., 19
Pennings, J. M., 16, 17, 24, 109
Perrow, Charles, xiii, 13, 15, 62, 122, 156, 163
Peters, Thomas J., 6, 14, 55, 117
Pettigrew, Andrew M., 17, 24
Pfeffer, Jeffrey, 16, 22, 24, 108, 145, 146, 158, 160
Pinchot, G., 6, 15
Piore, M. J., 14, 134, 138, 163
Pollock, A. B., 132, 168
Porter, Glenn, 26, 69, 72
Powell, Walter W., 21, 30, 161

Raskin, A. H., 23
Reskin, Barbara F., 52, 154
Roethlisberger, F. J., 60
Romeo, Anthony A., 37
Roos, Patricia A., 154, 166
Rosen, Corey, 130
Ross, Jerry, 145, 146
Rossow, Paula, xiii
Rowan, Brian, 21, 30, 161
Rubenstein, A. H., 23

Sabel, Charles F., 14, 20, 65, 123, 134, 138, 163
Salancik, Gerald, 16, 22, 24
Schneck, R. E., 16, 17, 24, 109
Schnorr, P., 26
Schumpeter, J. A., 16
Schwartz, Mildred A., xiii
Scott, J. T., 24, 37
Scott, W. Richard, 22, 132, 157
Selznick, Philip, 22, 23, 163
Shaiken, Harley, 20, 24, 90, 105, 159, 166
Simmons, John, 152
Simon, Herbert A., 14, 16, 21, 45, 56, 88, 113, 151, 166

Smith, Vicki, 152
Sorge, Arndt, 22
Stalker, G. M., 101
Starback, T. M. Jr., 127, 134, 136
Steiger, T., 52
Stinchcombe, Arthur L., xiii, 14, 25, 26, 91, 103, 148, 151, 158, 158, 165
Stone, K., 17
Strauss, A., 27
Streeck, Wolfgang, 22
Sullivan, Teresa, xiii

Taylor, Frederick W., 12, 138
Thomas, Robert J., 23, 29, 78, 146, 153, 158
Thompson, James D., 22, 80, 132, 156
Thompson, W. E., 80
Tolbert, Pamela S., 161
Trist, E. L., 132, 168
Tushman, Michael L., 62

Uetz, M. P., 109, 115, 118, 119, 141

Van de Ven, Andrew H., 161
Vollrath, D. A.,131

Walker, C. R., 134
Wallace, M., 43, 91, 166
Walsh, J. P., 26, 69, 81, 140, 155, 168
Wasserman, Marlie, xiii
Waterman, Robert H., 6, 14, 55, 117
Whalley, P., 19
Whyte, William F., 148, 168
Wilkinson, B., 22
Williamson, O. E., 14, 20, 25, 129
Wilson, James Q., 160
Wood, S., 22
Wozniak, Paul R., 145
Wright, J. Patrick, 111

Zetka, James, xiii
Zimbalist, A., 22
Zimmerman, M. M., 2, 47, 62, 92
Zuboff, S., 19, 20, 89–90, 105, 106, 155
Zucker, Lynne G., 21

SUBJECT INDEX

Ad Hoc Committee on Universal Product
    Codes, 94, 154, 164
Amalgamated Meat Cutters and Butcher
    Workmen of North America, 31–32, 82–
    83, 93. *See also* United Food and Com-
    mercial Workers
auto industry, 4, 23, 135
automation, 2, 20, 65, 90–92, 105–106, 166.
    See also scanners
autonomy, 13–16, 52, 60, 111–112, 116–
    122, 130–132, 139, 146–147, 149–151,
    155, 159, 168

bakeries, 1, 2, 9–11, 47, 51–52, 86–87, 108,
    118–146
bounded rationality, 14, 20–21, 105, 108,
    113–114
boxed beef, 77–85, 88, 155, 157, 158, 162.
    See also frozen meat; meat
    centralization
bundle of tasks, 27, 49, 88, 120, 133–136,
    140, 147, 150, 152, 155; low-status tasks,
    12, 27–28, 30, 63, 65, 85–87; meatcut-
    ters, 60–61, 82, 155; ordering, 2, 102–
    105, 106, 121–122, 126, 150, 154; service
    tasks, 86–87
bureaucratic control, 129–130
butchers. *See* meat cutters

carpenters, 28, 165
chain size. *See* firm size
chemical workers, 20

Chicago Tribune, 166
clothing industry, 163
computerized ordering, 2, 89, 102–105,
    106, 154–155, 158
construction, 162, 165
consumers, 22–23, 29–30, 63, 67–69, 87;
    and frozen meat, 73–76, 155; and self-
    serve meat, 67; and boxed beef, 83; and
    scanners, 5, 92–101, 154
contingency theory, 13, 15, 21, 161
convenience stores, 48–50
cultural changes, 2, 3, 18, 41, 45–46, 83;
    changing eating habits, 3, 46, 69

decentralization, 3, 13–15, 38, 52, 102–106,
    108–128, 146–148, 149–154, 155, 158,
    162–163
delis, 1, 2, 9–11, 47, 51, 85–87, 118–146,
    168
department heads, 9–11, 117, 126, 130–
    132, 150; duties, 7, 103, 107, 121–122,
    136, 140, 167; training, 134, 137; wages,
    127, 143–144, 167
deskilling, 12–13, 15, 19–20, 23, 28, 38,
    80–81, 88–90, 140, 155, 158
diversification strategy, 8, 9, 30, 51–56,
    85–88, 107, 110, 120, 146–148, 157
division of labor, 3, 7, 13, 17, 19, 20, 30, 54;
    hierarchical, 9, 12, 64, 68; hierarchical
    vs. nonhierarchical, 27–28, 88; in meat,
    60, 88; in management, 47, 103, 111
doctors, 27–28

electronic cash registers, 2, 95

firm size, 3, 4, 8, 18, 56–58, 114–116
Food Basket (supermarket), 1
food processing industry, 22, 92
frozen meat, 32, 72–77, 84, 88, 155, 157, 166, 168. *See also* boxed beef; meat centralization

gender: and deskilling, 80–81; job typing by, 34–35, 66, 111–112, 140, 167; and pay, 140–147, 152, 154, 163
General Motors, 109
Giant Foods (supermarket), 100
Grace (plastics maker), 78, 79
Gruppo GFT (clothing manufacturer), 163

health care, 162
Hobart (retail equipment), 95
hours, store, 3, 41, 48–51

IBM, 30
industrial districts, 138–139
inflation, 5, 92, 101
innovation, politicized context model of, 17–27, 68, 149, 156–160
institutional theory, 21, 30, 161
interdependence, 132
Iowa Beef Processors (IBP), 78–81, 84–85, 166

Kroger's (supermarket), 60

lettuce harvesting, 23, 78, 145–146, 153
local demand, 107, 110, 114–121, 163
longshoring, 20

machine tools, 4, 19–20, 22–23, 28, 158, 160, 166
managers, 3, 7–9, 33, 47, 52, 104, 108–113, 116–119, 138, 153–154
market context: decentralization, 108; and innovation, 19–21; meat centralization, 68–69; scanners, 91–92
market share (concentration), 71, 92; chains, 56; effects on innovation, 16; increasing, 3; packers, 70, 77, 84–85, 166; retailers, 70, 93

Marsh Supermarkets, 95–96
meat centralization, 2–3, 13, 26, 68–85, 155
meat cutters (butchers), 1, 7–8, 26–27, 59–88, 145, 167
meat saws 2, 61–62, 88
meat service, 60, 65–66, 119. *See also* self-service
meat wrappers (clerks), 1, 28, 65–68, 87–88
mechanization, 2, 13, 19, 30, 61–62, 87–88, 157
miners, 131
Minyard Food Store, 1
Missouri Beef, 78, 85
multidivisional form, 9, 14, 23, 109–110, 115, 129

NCR (cash register maker), 94–95
newspapers, 162, 166
nurses, 12

occupational culture, 153–154
one-stop-shopping. *See* diversification strategy
opportunism, 14, 107, 128–132, 150, 151
ordering. *See* bundle of tasks
organizational culture, 19, 151, 153
organizational environment, 3, 13–16, 21, 22, 37, 41, 63, 108, 149, 155, 156; munificence, 16, 18, 155; uncertainty, 13–15, 72, 80, 92
organizational innovation, causes, 12, 18–19, 41

painters, 28, 165
police, 26, 28
political contingencies: decentralization, 108–109; and innovation, 24–27; meat centralization, 69–71; scanners, 92–94. *See also* power
population growth, slowing, 2, 3, 32, 42–43
power, 16–17, 18, 23, 24–27, 58, 70, 82, 149, 158; effects of innovation on, 24, 71, 80, 83, 159–160; intrafirm, 108–109. *See also* political contingencies

prepared foods, 1, 3, 52, 115–116, 118–120
produce, 6, 41, 46, 121, 123, 126, 141–142
profit squeeze, 42–46, 48, 51, 91, 118; and
technological change, 32, 69

regional variation in markets, 36, 52, 56,
110, 114–116, 119–120, 150
restaurants, in store, 9, 119, 169
Retail Clerks International Union (RCIU),
31–32, 50, 93, 98. *See also* United Food
and Commercial Workers; unions
retail trade, economic importance of, 4,
32, 162

scanners, 2, 5, 16, 32, 89, 91–102, 106, 154–
155, 158–159, 162, 167
seafood shops, 1, 2, 9, 11, 47–48, 51, 85–
87, 108, 124, 126
Sears (retailer), 53, 55, 57, 115
self-service, 1, 2, 23, 47, 91; in meat, 62–
64, 67, 88
seniority, 34, 123, 127–128
service skill, 60–61, 63, 123–127, 133, 152;
and gender, 140–146; training, 86–87,
136–137
service strategy, 3, 9, 41, 45–52, 85–87,
123, 165
specialization, flexible, 14, 138
specialty shops, 1, 2, 3, 9, 51, 85, 118–146,
150
state, 146, 153, 162; and innovation, 23;
price marking legislation, 99–101; wage
and price controls, 5, 100, 162
statistical control, 129–130, 150, 163
steel industry, 4, 17
store size, 1–2, 3, 4, 7, 8, 43, 47, 52–55, 70;
and decentralization, 102–103, 110, 111,
150, 155; effects on innovation, 16, 91
suppliers, 22–23
Swift (meatpacker), 72–73, 76, 77

Taylorism, 30, 87–88, 138
teachers, 27
technological change, 2, 3, 12, 18, 19, 22,

32, 35, 41, 154, 155. *See also* automation;
computerized ordering; meat saws;
mechanization; scanners; wrap
machines

unions, 22–25, 31–32, 34, 86, 146, 154, 160,
161–162, 163–164, 165; and boxed beef,
70, 82; declining influence, 6, 101, 168;
and longer hours, 49–50; and scanners,
93, 98–101; work rules, 61, 65, 85, 113–
114. *See also* Amalgamated Meat Cutters; Retail Clerks; United Farm
Workers; United Food and Commercial
Workers
United Farm Workers, 29
United Food and Commercial Workers
(UFCW), 31–32, 34, 56, 57, 85, 93, 127,
165, 177. *See also* Amalgamated Meat
Cutters; Retail Clerks; unions

wages, 14, 42–43, 50, 66–67, 69, 86, 127,
140–146, 165, 168; two-tiered, 66, 168
Wetterau (wholesaler), 79
women workers, 3, 5, 45–46, 54, 75
worker ownership, 130, 168
worker participation, 6; quality circles, 15,
151; worker-management committees,
127–128
worker resistance, 6, 26–29; to boxed
beef, 81–85, 155, 157, 159; to division of
labor, 28; lack of, 51, 62–68, 76, 86, 104,
147, 159; to scanners, 5, 92–95, 98–101,
154, 157, 159
worker skill, 13–16, 24, 56, 107, 118–127,
132–140, 147, 163; and decentralization,
14–15, 117; in meat, 59–66, 69–70; ordering, 105, 121–122, 126; specialty
shops, 11, 51
worker status, 12, 26–28, 60–61, 66–67,
85, 140–147, 150, 152–153, 163
worker training, 132–140, 147, 150, 151;
formal, 136–139
wrap machines (meat), 2, 64–65

The Rose Monograph Series was established in 1968 in honor of the distinguished sociologists Arnold and Caroline Rose whose bequest makes the Series possible. The sole criterion for publication in the Series is that a manuscript contribute to knowledge in the discipline of sociology in a systematic and substantial manner. All areas of the discipline and all established and promising modes of inquiry are equally eligible for consideration. The Rose Monograph Series is an official publication of the American Sociological Association.

Editor: Teresa A. Sullivan

Editorial Board

Lewis F. Carter
Helen Rose Ebaugh
Anthony M. Orum

Dudley L. Poston, Jr.
Michael Schudson
Russell Thornton

SUPERMARKETS TRANSFORMED

THE ARNOLD AND CAROLINE ROSE MONOGRAPH SERIES
OF THE AMERICAN SOCIOLOGICAL ASSOCIATION